Praise for *Your Health Is at Risk*

This book is a must-read for anyone who cares about their health. It offers truthful understanding about serious matters of health and merits our most sincere attention. We are currently overwhelmed with disinformation and misinformation from a variety of sources, so it is crucial that we establish the credibility of whatever we read, see, or hear. Failing to do so can harm us and those we love. This book is the best of its kind and will help you avoid mistakes that besiege healthcare regarding diabetes, cancer, heart disease, and pandemics.

—Dr. Venugopal Menon, MD, FAAP, FAAA&I, FACAA&I,
Fellow of the Royal Society of Medicine, London

As a broadcaster, I've covered the consequences of disinformation and misinformation highlighted especially in the federal government's response to the COVID-19 pandemic. Dr. John's timely examination of DMMI is crucial to making informed, accurate decisions about your health.

—Matt Ray, Host of *America's First News* Radio Program

Very interesting and informative book . . . extremely relevant in the age of pandemics and social media! A must read for anyone in media or healthcare, as well as anyone interested in their own health.

—Aakash Aggarwal, MD, Affiliated Faculty,
Gastroenterology, Hackensack University Medical Center

Extremely engaging book, which addresses the very contemporary issue of disinformation in the healthcare sector in the era of widespread social media use. It contains practical advice on how to get the right kind of healthcare literacy as well as preventive health measures. . . great read!'

—Jyoti Sharma, MD, Palliative care,
Memorial Sloan Kettering Cancer Center

YOUR HEALTH IS AT RISK

YOUR HEALTH IS AT RISK

HOW TO NAVIGATE INFORMATION CHAOS TO PREVENT LIFESTYLE DISEASES

Pandemics, Type 2 Diabetes, Cancer, Cardiovascular Disease

JOHN M. POOTHULLIL, MD, FRCP

NEW INSIGHTS PRESS

IMPORTANT NOTICE: This book is not intended to replace the medical treatment of any disease or illness. It presents the author's insights regarding lifestyle conditions such as pandemics, Type 2 diabetes, cancer, and cardiovascular disease. Consult a medical professional for specific diagnostic information and treatment.

Editorial Direction and Editing: Rick Benzel
Copyediting: Julie Simpson, OnWords and UpWords!
Cover and Book Design: Susan Shankin
Cover Illustration: Tim Kummerow
Published by New Insights Press, Los Angeles, CA

First edition printed in the United States of America

ISBN: 978-1-7359344-7-1

Library of Congress Control Number: 2021920566

Do not accept any of my words on faith,
believing them just as I said them.
Be like an analyst buying gold, who cuts,
burns, and critically
examines his product for authenticity.
Only accept what passes the test by proving useful
and beneficial in your life.

— Siddhartha Gautama, the Buddha

CONTENTS

	Introduction	xi
CHAPTER 1	Donald Trump and Disinformation about the Covid-19 Pandemic	1
CHAPTER 2	Misinformation about Type 2 Diabetes	41
CHAPTER 3	Missing Information about Body Weight, Diets, and Eating for Nutrition	79
CHAPTER 4	Missing Information about Cancer	101
CHAPTER 5	The Role of Mixed DMMI in Cardiovascular Disease	121
CHAPTER 6	Strategies to Prevent DMMI from Influencing Your Health Decisions	137
	Epilogue	179
	Appendix: Questions to Ask Your Doctor	185
	Endnotes	189
	About the Author	191

INTRODUCTION

When we look at medicine and healthcare today, there is clearly a divide between wonderful news and bad news. On one hand, each year seems to bring new progress in the prevention and treatment of various diseases and conditions. Researchers and care providers in every field of medicine are advancing their knowledge and skills. Innovations in the design, manufacturing, and capabilities of medical equipment lower costs and advance efficacies of increasingly powerful machines and faster execution of tests and procedures used in patient care.

On the other hand is another side to the story: *information chaos*. People are overwhelmed with information, but what is the worst side of this is that medicine and healthcare today are increasingly tainted by *disinformation, misinformation*, or *missing information* (which I will henceforth refer to collectively as DMMI). These factors may be preventing you from maintaining your health and even contributing to making you less healthy than you could be. DMMI may often mislead you to make incorrect decisions based on your perceptions of lifestyle conditions such as pandemic viruses, Type 2 diabetes, cancer, and heart disease.

To be clear, in the context of health information and the choices people make about their healthcare, the three issues of DMMI are distinctly different:

- **Disinformation** is the intentional, conscious, and often malicious effort to provide false information or the wrong data about health issues to mislead people for one reason or another. Sometimes disinformation stems from a company's vested interest in making money, which leads it to make false claims about the value of a medicine, supplement, or medical procedure. Other times, disinformation comes from a source that has vested interests in promoting its own social or political policies or stances on a topic. The key characteristic of disinformation is that it is provably false but repetition makes it appear as if it is the truth.
- **Misinformation** refers to the unintentional promulgation of wrong information that misleads people into making poor health decisions. Misinformation may come from a poorly-informed source that lacks knowledge, skills, or training on a health issue and therefore promotes information that is contrary to accurate scientific facts. Some people might question who determines what is "accurate," but if the scientific consensus based on measurable, verifiable, and replicable research is consistent, it should be accepted as the correct information.
- **Missing information** is incomplete information, resulting from a situation in which those in charge of the information have not obtained or given out all the information that might help people make the right healthcare decisions for themselves and their loved ones. On the one hand, some available information may have been withheld, or, on the other hand, the existence of additional information may not have been known. The recipient, unaware that information is missing, will act based on his or her belief in what was available regarding a medical procedure, treatment, use of a drug or supplement, diet, or any other health-related choice. Unlike disinformation, missing information is neither intentional nor malicious; unlike misinformation, it is not accidentally incorrect.

We may see a mixture of DMMI when there is a combination of two or three of these problems in the delivery of information related to a health condition. It can be extremely difficult to separate out the many factors that may cause you to make bad healthcare decisions. Your knowledge of a medical subject may include some disinformation, some misinformation, and some missing information—all of which lead you to have incorrect knowledge on a topic and/or make poor choices in how you decide to live your life.

In this book, my goal is to show how information chaos in the form of DMMI has a tremendous impact on how people make their health decisions. In my view, there are numerous illnesses and conditions, as well as diet beliefs and eating behaviors, where DMMI plays a key role in leading people to make wrong and unhealthy choices. It is increasingly difficult, in fact, to escape from DMMI today, given how much people are now surrounded by information not only from their doctors and medical professionals, but from an infinite variety of media sources—television, internet, social media, newspapers, AM/FM radio, cable networks, audiobooks, podcasts, and more. Worse, most people have little training in how to understand and analyze what they see and hear when it comes to health and lifestyle topics. They may be easily pulled into believing disinformation, do not recognize misinformation, and do not have the ability to detect when they might be missing information. In this book, I intend to be your advocate.

"Health Illiteracy" Is Rising

Literacy usually refers to the ability to read and write at a level high enough to function as an adult in life. The non-profit organization ProLiteracy cites that 43 million Americans cannot read, write, or do basic math above a 3rd grade level. Between the years 2000 and 2017, 10% of adults 25 years old and older did not complete their high school education. This translates to more than 23 million Americans who have less than a 12th grade education.

ProLiteracy correlates the lack of literacy among U.S. adults with significant consequences in healthcare. They state, "It is estimated between $106–$238 billion in healthcare costs a year are linked to low adult literacy skills. Adults with limited health literacy are hospitalized and use emergency services at significantly higher rates than those with higher skills."[1]

The drawbacks of illiteracy and low literacy are just one element in the DMMI problem, however. We must also recognize that even literate adults can lack another key life skill when it comes to understanding information: critical thinking. This term refers to the ability to analyze whatever one reads to determine if it is logical or illogical, reasonable or unreasonable, rational or irrational, and likely to be true or false. Critical thinking involves noticing the flow of an argument, whether valid evidence is presented, and if the conclusions drawn from that evidence make sense. Good critical thinking also compares whatever the person reads or hears with other knowledge they have obtained in the past so they can assess if it jives with the reality they know. It also examines who the speaker or writer is, whether they have credibility in that field, or are faking their expertise.

For purposes of this book therefore, when I talk about health illiteracy, I am referring to the deficit of either NOT being able to read and write at a high school level or NOT having critical thinking skills even though one might be literate. Both types of skills are necessary for making good health choices based on good information, as well as being able to detect DMMI.

It should be noted that a lack of literacy and critical thinking skill is not necessarily the individual's fault. Circumstances in one's family and/or society at large are often the root cause of illiteracy. Poverty, for example, is known to take a toll on a child's educational drive and opportunities. Children who grow up in poverty often lack access to good schools and other resources to achieve literacy. Parents may not be literate themselves and so lack the ability to foster reading and thinking skills in their children. Communities with high levels of poverty usually lack the funds and facilities to support high quality educational systems that encourage children to read or even to complete high school.

Poverty can also greatly affect brain development. Inadequate access to good food that supplies the necessary nutrients for growth, especially during infancy and childhood, can have a negative and lasting effect on intellectual capacity. Stress in the home or community environment during the critical childhood formative years could create the same outcome.

Also contributing to health illiteracy is the fact that only a small percentage of people in the world have had a reasonably in-depth education in the sciences of biology, chemistry, nutrition, or health. Most adults have not taken a science class since they were in middle or high school, and that can be decades ago. Meanwhile the science and healthcare fields have advanced by leaps and bounds. I have written four books—two on diabetes and two on cancer—and I am constantly reminded by my editor that I have to dial back the amount of science I use to demonstrate my new insights into diabetes and cancer because people won't want to read too much science or understand it if they do.

Even among the college-educated, understanding the chemistry of glucose utilization, how organs work, the nature of stem cells, basic biological facts about diabetes and cancer, or the details of how pandemics get started can be daunting. In other words, as my editor tells me, people are generally unenthusiastic about learning the science underlying their medical conditions. But that is what I hope to change, so I hope you will read on. If you want to defeat DMMI from causing you to make detrimental lifestyle choices, it is truly worth your time and effort to read this book and take in the brief science education I can offer you.

The Consequences of Health Illiteracy

A literate person in today's world is aware that the traditional media and social media are swarming with intentional disinformation about many topics, from politics to finances, to health advice and diet plans. Literacy, critical thinking, and a tolerance for reading scientific material are absolutely necessary to detect such disinformation.

Let me cite some consequences of health illiteracy and low levels of science education. Thousands of scams abound to persuade people to purchase fake or non-existent products or services or to convince them to follow some type of expensive diet or to believe in a fake cure. People with insufficient literacy can be susceptible to such disinformation; they may not have had enough of a background to distinguish between fact and fiction, and/or they cannot critically analyze what they read or hear to detect that it is illogical, unscientific, or just plain nonsense.

Disinformation can appear to be real and accurate, but people with literacy and critical thinking skills are able to recognize when they are being deceived. The clues to disinformation may be obvious to some, such as misspelled or missing words in an advertisement or a gaping hole in the logic of a presentation. But without a sufficient background in language and logic, such clues would not be evident. Disinformation can also be subtly disguised and hard to detect by even the most literate. However, most people with the ability to think critically know to read the media with a certain skepticism and are hesitant to believe something without more research and additional proof. People with enough education and life experience also know how to evaluate if what they read seems implausible or unreasonable compared to what they already know.

The devastating effect of disinformation can be seen in the handling of the pandemic caused by the novel coronavirus, Covid-19, that was alleged to have been first detected in Wuhan, China in December 2019. When the outbreak began, the provincial and central Chinese governments started a sustained campaign of disinformation to hide the severity of the disease and the possibility that it could become a pandemic, even as the infection spread quickly inside China and out into the entire world through tourism and business travelers.

But China was not alone in the use of disinformation. In the United States, in the early months of the spread of the virus, then-President Donald Trump intentionally and repeatedly spread disinformation about it. This was either because of his inability to fully grasp the gravity of the worst public health crisis in a century, or because, ever the showman, he sought to project the appearance of being in total control of the crisis in order to ensure he would win reelection. His stance on the pandemic encouraged conservative leaders to refuse to act and their followers to view federal regulations and efforts to curb the virus spread as infringements on their personal liberty.

The result was that during just the first five days of December 2020, there were 1 million new Covid-19 cases in the USA whereas it took three months for the virus to reach the first one million people stricken in the early stages of the pandemic. How and why this happened and its consequences in terms of the hundreds of thousands of lives that could have been saved are explained in further detail later in this book.

The point is, millions of U.S. citizens who supported President Trump believed his disinformation campaign, and in 2021 we saw the consequences of this in the politicization of mask-wearing and lagging vaccination rates. As I write this book, it is now being said that Covid-19 has become a Republican disease, since it is largely in the "red" states of the country, those with Republican governors, where the highest rates of infection and death continue to occur. This is due largely to disinformation about such things as the method of spread of Covid-19 virus, the protective effects of wearing face masks, and the vital importance of being vaccinated. As the Delta and Omicron variants of the virus are more easily transmitted, we are seeing, as this book is published, a new surge of cases, hospitalizations, and deaths—a "pandemic of the unvaccinated."

Turning from the topic of disinformation to that of **misinformation**, the need for literacy when it comes to misinformation is also clear. What may not be clear are the *causes* of the spread of misinformation. For example, widespread dissemination of misinformation can be caused by the unintentional *misinterpretation* of scientific evidence collected during research and verification of an original hypothesis about an illness or disease. This can then cascade down to individuals and organizations with vested interests in promoting the wrong information.

Misinformation can also result from the constant updating of information that happens in medical and biological sciences. While it is a common practice in these fields to change established theories and practices when new information becomes available or when old interpretations need to be updated due to newly uncovered evidence, many health organizations, medical professionals, and companies selling products or services may simply continue delivering out-of-date information to the public either intentionally or without realizing the need to update. I will explain in this book, for instance, why I believe that the diagnosis and treatment of Type 2 diabetes is an example of this.

Another cause of misinformation is the inability of recipients to recognize when they are receiving it. This requires an individual to have a proactive, inquiring mind; they must first suspect they have received misinformation and then decide to look into it further. Those who are prone to accepting things at face value are more likely to accept misinformation unknowingly.

Misinformation can be detrimental when people don't understand a critical aspect of a health topic. They will act on whatever they think is the right course of action, unaware that they don't have a thorough understanding of the issue. Studies have documented the degree to which communication from healthcare providers is frequently too complex to be understandable for many patients and their families. This applies to both written and verbal communication. Although providers themselves may be partially at fault for this problem, the lack of a high level of literacy among patients probably plays a larger role.

Another factor in the cause of health misinformation is fear. People who are diagnosed with certain diseases or illnesses can become afraid of a dire outcome, and thus too eager to find information that gives them hope. This can lead to an unhealthy dependence on unreliable sources and remedies. Making the most reliable and up-to-date information about certain diseases available to patients has resulted in the formation of many global, national, and local health associations.

These organizations attempt to assure the public that they are receiving accurate, complete, and easy-to-understand information on their disease or condition. One assumes that these organizations are dedicated to providing factual information, but this may not always be the case, as this book will attest in some of the chapters. Some of these so-called non-profit educational organizations are more about self-promotion than about presenting accurate scientific information.

As for **missing information**, the issue here is that illiteracy and a poor science background make it very hard for people to intuit or sense that they might be missing something about a topic. The information may appear to be complete on the surface, but without at least some pre-existing understanding of the subject or the related science, people will accept what they read or hear as the entire story and make decisions based on that. In addition, this void creates an opportunity for alternate explanations and interpretations to enter into someone's conception of the issue, making them gullible to "feel good" remedies.

For example, I believe that people often accept a course of action recommended by their doctors when it comes to treatments for cardiovascular disease and cancer, despite missing some important information, as I will explain in this book. In short, if people cannot read or fully understand the medical instructions they receive, and don't take the initiative to ask critical questions, they risk making healthcare decisions based on incomplete information.

How to Prevent DMMI from Harming Your Health Decisions and Lifestyle Choices

Let me be clear. My reason for writing this book is not to assign blame. My goal is to be a patient advocate and shed light on how DMMI can lead millions of people to make poor or wrong choices concerning lifestyle decisions about such things as diet and eating habits, as well as the treatment of several diseases. In today's world, the average person is inundated with information about scores of medical and health issues, both significant and insignificant. Information abounds regarding everything from chronic life-threatening illnesses to theories on nutrition, offering dietary supplements and various methods and "workarounds" to lose weight, gain more energy, and on and on. We now also have pharmaceutical companies advertising their medicines directly to consumers, seeking to convince them to go to their doctors and insist on receiving the advertised drug.

These factors—insufficient science background or training combined with a broad level of health illiteracy and lack of critical thinking skills among the general public—make it common now for millions of people to be duped by health disinformation, while others make critical health choices affecting their lives based on misinformation or missing information. My hope is that this book can raise awareness of DMMI and thereby contribute to preventing it from becoming increasingly common in people's decision-making process about their lifestyle and health.

The Evolution of DMMI in the Media

The media plays a significant role in the spread of DMMI, particularly disinformation. Perhaps one of the most destructive and powerful examples of this in recent history is the rise of Adolph Hitler and Nazism that began in Germany after World War 1. Actions taken by the victorious Allied Powers left Germany impoverished and Germans deprived. Using the media (newspapers and radio), Hitler was able to convince ordinary Germans that Germany was not really defeated, but that a conspiracy by Jews and socialists was responsible for the Armistice and the perceived surrender of Germany. Hitler very effectively kept spreading this view to people who were suffering from economic depression through a multitude of communication platforms with the intention of creating anger directed against the affluent, especially Jews.

Another example is the rise of a Communist state after Marxist ideology spread like wildfire among poor Russians who took out their frustrations against a dictatorial, tyrannical Tsarist regime.

Today's social media has significantly altered the power of traditional media to influence people. Although started as a forum to connect and share with friends, social media not only informs and entertains but also raises curiosity that is fed by new ideas for creating content to satisfy the increasing need for information. This has led to the spread of information based less on facts than on fiction that is disguised or interpreted as fact.

The inability to distinguish fact from fiction has furthermore led to creative ways in which some people knowingly manipulate the reach of the media to obtain a certain outcome. The result is that it is now possible for almost anyone in any part of the world to have access to the opinions expressed by others without having to be present in the immediate vicinity. This has also created an opportunity for like-minded people who accept only what they believe in to join together not only to share information but also to project strength in numbers.

This means that for anyone to acquire factual knowledge, he or she has to not only have the opportunity to get the input and the capability to screen it, but also the capacity to deal with it efficiently. The efficiency of understanding, the learning curve, as some people call it, is greatly influenced by the circumstances under which the input is received and the number of repetitions and time needed for the individual to encode it in memory. Keep in mind that people make judgments based on their understanding of information received from those in charge. Disinformation makes them susceptible to feel-good interventions, especially when the leader guarantees an outcome satisfactory to all who follow his or her directions.

The above-mentioned vulnerability makes it possible for an influential group to promote unscientific explanations and remedies and/or to color data in a way that diminishes the gravity of a situation or enhances the value of feel-good advice. This is done essentially to manipulate and shape the thought processes of those who are willing to believe. The followers may believe even fragmented information coming out of a trusted source, especially when they are anxious and panicking.

This tendency could attract and empower other groups to use the same platform to further their own vested interests, even if they are not scientifically proven to have the desired benefit. I call this the "resonance" effect because instead of using the media to amplify proven remedies, determined people use the social media platforms to spread disinformation, misinformation, and partial information to change the behavior of followers, as well as to enrich themselves.

Those who recognize the true nature of half-truths may remain tolerant and silent even after repeatedly hearing a falsehood promoted by the perceived "authority." They do not speak up perhaps because they feel that it is not worth the effort, assuming that, sooner or later, someone may produce evidence to the contrary. This highlights the critical role of scientists who have not confronted the spread in social media of disinformation, misinformation, and missing information related to healthcare. This failure to monitor and correct such information has allowed digital media to be a platform for creation, reception, sharing, and spreading of disinformation, misinformation, and partial information on a societal level. What experts thought of as "temporary" can be sustained by a core group of individuals determined to take advantage of the opportunity for private gain.

It is also important to recognize how quickly DMMI can spread among an entire population or among a closely knit group with vested interests in something other than scientific truth. Equally important is to appreciate the fact that it is difficult to completely erase any DMMI that has been propagated, even when evidence dictates otherwise.

The Organization of this Book

It is not difficult to find disinformation, misinformation, or missing information regarding almost every medical condition. There is folklore and superstition about nearly every disease in the world to some degree or another.

Instead of enumerating each and every instance of DMMI in a variety of conditions, each chapter of this book uses one specific condition to illustrate one of the issues of DMMI.

- Chapter 1 discusses the topic of disinformation as it relates to pandemics.
- Chapter 2 delves into Type 2 diabetes as the prime example of misinformation.
- Chapter 3 covers missing information about maintaining your weight, avoiding weight gain and obesity, and the problems with weight-loss diets.
- Chapter 4 covers cancer as another example of missing information.
- Chapter 5 shows how we are frequently under a mix of both misinformation *and* missing information about the role of high cholesterol, whole grains, and salt in our understanding of cardiovascular conditions (heart disease).
- In Chapter 6, I present my recommendations for measures that readers can take to avoid falling for DMMI in making their healthcare decisions.
- In the Appendix, I provide questions that you can ask your doctor about the lifestyle conditions covered in the chapters of this book. The goal of these questions is not to embarrass your doctor but to help you gain a clearer understanding of the real medical science about your condition and its treatment.

> However, some of these questions may challenge your doctor to also question whether what he or she believes is accurate. This is potentially an opportunity for your doctor to update his or her knowledge on the topic and even to rethink your treatment plan. Doctors are not right all the time, and sometimes patients must challenge them to go deeper in their understanding of the cause of a lifestyle condition and how best to help you prevent or eliminate it.

Beyond the scope of this book, and thus not discussed here, are such topics as the impact of misdirection of propaganda for profit that promotes ideas in the areas of cigarette smoking, and alcohol and drug use. I also do not discuss the misguided promotion of ideas based on political beliefs about "liberty" versus "government authority," ideas which drive some amount of disinformation concerning the prevention of Covid-19 through such measures as vaccinations, masks, and social distancing protocols, as well as treatments. Also not within the scope of this book is the promotion of health and drug insurance plans for profit, where there is often DMMI.

DMMI is making people ill with lifestyle conditions that they could have prevented if they could recognize the disinformation and misinformation or the missing information. DMMI has become an enemy of public health and we must do something about it. I hope you take the message of this book seriously, discuss it with your healthcare providers and even promote it to your community and political representatives in government.

Introduction Takeaways

- Medicine and healthcare today are increasingly tainted by disinformation, misinformation, or missing information (which I refer to collectively as DMMI). These factors may be preventing you from maintaining your health and even contributing to making you less healthy than you could be. DMMI may often mislead you to make incorrect decisions based on your perceptions of lifestyle conditions such as pandemic viruses, Type 2 diabetes, cancer, and heart disease.
- Thousands of scams abound to persuade people to purchase fake or non-existent products or services or to convince them to follow some type of expensive diet or to believe in a fake cure. People with insufficient literacy can be susceptible to DMMI because they may not have had enough of a background to distinguish between fact and fiction, and/or they cannot critically analyze what they read or hear to detect that it is illogical, unscientific, or just plain nonsense. If you want to defeat DMMI from causing you to make detrimental lifestyle choices, it is truly worth your time and effort to read this book to take in the brief science education I can offer you.
- Today's social media has significantly altered the power of traditional media to influence people. Social media not only informs and entertains but is now also a prime source for information based less on facts than on fiction. It is now possible for almost anyone in any part of the world to express an opinion on a health or medical topic without any expertise or scientific facts to support it.

CHAPTER 1

DONALD TRUMP AND DISINFORMATION ABOUT THE COVID-19 PANDEMIC

We are increasingly witnessing intentional disinformation appearing in the media about many health issues. It often comes from vendors of fake cures who, like the traveling snake oil salesmen of the old Wild West, promote their unproven and useless products in magazine ads and on social media. However, never have we seen the depth and quantity of disinformation than has been promoted about the coronavirus pandemic. This disinformation came from many sources including but not limited to China and former President Donald J. Trump. This chapter focuses largely on the role that President Trump played in a misguided effort to use disinformation for his own political goals.

There can be NO question that, no matter what else one might think of Donald Trump as President, he failed when it comes to the pandemic. He intentionally used false facts and misled the American people in their healthcare decisions. Trump, to his credit, made available to the research community both finances and other resources needed to develop the vaccines to stem the spread of Covid-19, without which the country could not have had any hope of ever controlling the pandemic. However, it is more likely that another president may have treated the pandemic more seriously and taken every precaution to avoid doling out disinformation as Mr. Trump consistently did. This chapter reviews the role of his intentional disinformation campaign that damaged the country's ability to handle the pandemic and led to hundreds of thousands of unnecessary deaths.

IT HAS BEEN well established that nearly 75% of all new, emerging, or re-emerging virus-based diseases affecting humans at the beginning of the 21st century are diseases that normally exist in wild animals and jump to humans. The mechanism that allows the jump is a mutation that occurs in the genes of the virus. The mutation usually occurs when the animal's immune system attempts to fight off the agent and, in response, the infectious agent adapts itself for its own survival. Then, in its slightly revised genetic form, the infection is able to survive in another creature that might be living nearby or that comes into close contact with the original infected animal. That creature might be a different animal who then has close contact with a human being who catches the infection.

Some infectious agents like viruses that undergo mutations do not survive for long and end up posing no problems for animals or humans. For example, the U.S. Centers for Disease Control and Prevention regularly tracks and reports on cases of new strains of influenza infecting people who attend county fairs as well as infecting animals such as pigs. These events are probably happening often, but if the virus is not lucky enough to find enough people interacting in a densely packed environment, the virus dies out. In fact, over 70% of such infections are thought to be the fate of most viruses.

However, some mutations allow the organism to pack itself into a tighter and lighter configuration capable of staying airborne longer, traveling farther and spreading wider than the original version. This is known as aerosol spreading, as opposed to droplet spreading in which the size of the viral particle is larger and falls to the ground or onto surfaces that other animals or humans touch. It is also important to understand virus mutation does not stop with entry to the human body. In fact, mutation continues, possibly inside each human, creating copies of the virus slightly different in structure and capability compared to the parent virus, as will be discussed later.

I am suggesting that pandemics should actually be considered lifestyle diseases. This may seem strange to say, given that we know the root cause of a pandemic is a virus or bacterium. But I consider pandemics to be lifestyle illnesses because they would not occur if people did not live a certain lifestyle that facilitates their spread. For example, if one person gets a virus and does not leave their house, they are unlikely to spread the virus to others. Some members of their household may develop it, and even perhaps some neighbors, relatives, or friends who visit, but the virus can remain rather contained and not become a pandemic—i.e., a worldwide disease—if people did not travel, go shopping, visit other families, or leave their homes to go to work or conduct business. The best evidence to support this notion that the novel coronavirus pandemic should be considered a lifestyle illness is the fact that the virus spread globally as humans traveled from place to place using all available transportation systems.

Pandemic History

The history of humanity has many examples of pandemics that have killed millions of people many times in the past. Consider the following:

Tuberculosis: Tuberculosis (TB) is an infectious disease caused by Mycobacterium tuberculosis bacteria. TB is closely linked to overcrowding, poverty, and malnutrition. It is believed that human tuberculosis started even before the Neolithic revolution from an unknown source. Tuberculosis spreads among humans via respiratory droplets from one person to the next through the air, especially when people who have active TB in their lungs cough, spit, speak, or sneeze.

The Plague: The best-known pandemic, the Plague, is also called the Black Death. It occurred several times in the 14th century and resulted in more than 50 million deaths. The Plague is not a virus but a bacterium that enters the body when a flea bites, introducing the bacteria into the tissue. It can then spread among humans via airborne droplets that contain bacterial cells coming out of the lungs, especially when an infected person coughs. The Plague still occurs from time to time in our modern era.

Smallpox: A smallpox pandemic was recorded in 18th-century Europe. It most likely was an African rodent virus that mutated between 68,000 and 16,000 years ago and became capable of infecting humans.

Influenza (1918 Spanish flu): This strain of the H1N1 influenza A virus, which became known as the Spanish flu, was estimated to have caused between 17 million and 50 million deaths worldwide in the 1918 pandemic. Based on the similarity of the strain, it is believed that the virus originally passed from birds to pigs living on farms and then infected humans.

The Novel Coronavirus Known as Covid-19

According to The World Health Organization (WHO), SARS-CoV-2 is the official name of the virus that causes the disease we know as Covid-19. That stands for "severe acute respiratory syndrome coronavirus 2." The term COVID stands for "coronavirus disease" and the "19" refers to the year 2019, when it first appeared in humans. In the interest of simplicity, in this book I use the term "Covid-19 virus" to refer to the virus itself and "Covid-19" to refer to the disease caused by that virus.

It has been clearly established that among humans, the Covid-19 virus that was first detected in 2019 spread via respiratory droplets coming out of the lungs. Several months after its emergence, it was found that Covid-19 spread most easily by airborne droplets, which explained the rapid increase in "community spread," whereby people who were not in direct physical contact with anyone who had Covid-19 developed the infection just by breathing the air that a person carrying the virus had expelled in that area.

It is believed that the virus that causes Covid-19 originated in bats and spread first to another animal and then to humans. The closest-known relatives to the coronavirus were collected from bats in China's Yunnan province in 2012-2013 and in 2019. However, out of 30,000 nucleotides that are the building blocks of the virus, the bat virus is still 1,200 nucleotides different.

The first outbreak of Covid-19 was reported in a Wuhan market, 1000 miles away from Yunnan province. It is conceivable that if the first human infected with the virus had been too sick to travel to Wuhan, we may not have had a Covid-19 pandemic. The Wuhan market had 635 stalls selling live animals such as chipmunks, foxes, racoons, wild boar, giant salamanders, hedgehogs, sike deer, snakes, frogs, quail, bamboo rats, rabbits, crocodiles, and badgers in addition to meat, seafood, fruits, and vegetables. In short, it was a place of close contact among animals and great activity of people from many regions of China, an ideal ground for virus spread.

Some scientists believe that the virus infected pangolins (a scaled-covered mammal) that were sold in the market near the bats, as they were found to have a form of the coronavirus with 91% of its identity similar to that of the bats. Some scientists have alternatively suggested other animal species may have been the intermediate host. However, other scientists have suggested that the origin may have been outside China, though they have not offered any meaningful evidence of that theory. Still others point to a specific government laboratory that was researching coronaviruses and was located near the market.

The Wuhan market was closed right after the outbreak began, in a rush to disinfect, as some environmental samples from the market contained viruses matching those in patients who became ill. But could the virus have come to Wuhan in a different way, that is, not through the market? A study of 41 confirmed cases from Wuhan showed that nearly 70% had been in contact with the market; however, 30% had not, including three of the first four cases.

The question of the virus's precise origin will be answered only by genetic sequencing to chart how the virus moved from one animal to another and to humans. This exercise is still going on at this writing.

Disinformation – Chinese Style

The earliest known case of the Covid-19 coronavirus was identified on December 1, 2019, according to a February 2020 study by Chinese researchers published in the medical journal, *Lancet.*[2] On December 24, 2019, Wuhan Central Hospital sent a bronchoalveolar lavage fluid (BAL) sample from an unresolved clinical case to the gene sequencing company, Vision Medicals. On December 27 and 28, Vision Medicals informed Wuhan Central Hospital and the Chinese agency that is the equivalent of the U.S. CDC that they identified a new coronavirus, similar to the prior coronaviruses of SARS and MERS. The virus is called coronavirus because of the crown-like spikes that appear around the surfaces of each virus.

Chinese authorities first alerted the World Health Organization (WHO) on December 31, 2019, that an unidentified pneumonia was spreading in Wuhan, but they were sure it was "preventable and controllable." At the same time, however, Chinese social media censors started deleting any references to an unknown pneumonia connected to the "Wuhan Seafood Market," "Wuhan unknown pneumonia," or "SARS variation."

One might say that this was the beginning of an intentional Chinese disinformation campaign. On January 1, 2020, Li Wenliang, a doctor in Wuhan, was forced to sign an apology for making "false statements" regarding a SARS-like virus in Wuhan to a group of fellow doctors inside a WeChat group. In addition, eight doctors were punished for "spreading rumors about an unknown pneumonia" after discussing the virus in private group texts.

It has also been reported that several other Chinese truth tellers who wanted to share with the world how slow authorities were to warn the public and the world of the coronavirus threat paid a heavy price for their work, with some being detained in prison and others gone missing. Chinese authorities sentenced one journalist to jail for reporting and publishing videos from Wuhan showing life under the pandemic lockdown.

Meanwhile, on January 1, 2020, Wuhan authorities were shutting down the Wuhan market. Although it was later revealed that about one-third of the Covid-19 cases in the first cluster of infections had no connection to the market, pointing to an origin elsewhere, Beijing continued to identify the market as the clear source of the outbreak. The government quickly emptied and sanitized the market, but they also later claimed that they didn't take enough biological samples, thus ensuring it would be difficult for later investigators to prove the connection.

On January 14, 2020, talking on a private conference call, Chinese Health Minister Ma Xiaowei reportedly called the virus "the most severe challenge since SARS in 2003" and said that "clustered cases suggest that human-to-human transmission is possible."[3] Yet, Beijing did not alert the WHO, the U.S., or any other countries of this change in emphasis regarding the contagious nature of the virus. According to the *Washington Post*, as reported on January 28, 2021, throughout January 2020 official Chinese authorities continued declaring that "no clear evidence shows human-to-human transmission" —even as victims were dying in the streets.

It is possible that Chinese authorities believed that they could still contain the virus and prevent widespread dissemination of the infection, despite the fact that the virus was spreading via respiratory droplets, as most viruses do. They may not have anticipated or really appreciated the potential disaster with the aerosol mode of spread.

Equally important is the fact that Chinese scientists were not aware, at that time, of the role of "silent spread," also known as asymptomatic transmission, meaning transmission of the virus from an infected person before he or she even exhibits symptoms. Asymptomatic transmission is a major contributing factor to creating the conditions for a global pandemic, as it occurs without anyone's knowledge of it during normal human interactions in closed environments such as while traveling, attending religious services or political events, during formal and informal gatherings, or in any other indoor group event.

What was worse, however, is that in January 2020 and much of February, China prevented American and international investigators from entering the country to investigate the origin of the virus. Even when they were allowed entry in late February 2020, experts were not given appropriate access to conduct a thorough examination, including interviews with Chinese scientists in China, access to biological samples from the laboratory in Wuhan, and opportunities to assess personal experience data of the laboratory workers. Just as they had done during the SARS epidemic, the Chinese authorities executed an effective campaign to present a false picture to its own people and the world. Why?

The most obvious reason was to prevent financial ruin for many inhabitants of the Wuhan region in the early months of 2020. To understand this, you need to know about the key importance of the Spring Festival—the Lunar New Year celebration. Celebrated in all of China, the Spring Festival is comparable to Thanksgiving, Christmas, or the Super Bowl in the United States. For many years, the main force behind China's fast economic growth has been rural migrant workers, estimated at around 288.36 million in 2018, who come home from the major cities for reunion with family and friends during the holiday. To celebrate, families substantially increase their spending on food, drink, and entertainment.

In 2018, the national retail and catering revenues had risen 10.2%, and even greater increases were expected year after year. China's film industry is also at its busiest when it caters to the need for entertainment at this time of the year. Also, the 40-day travel period that runs from January 10 until February 18 is the busiest period for rail and air travel. In 2020, the Chinese authorities projected 440 million passengers travelling by rail and 79 million travelling by air, setting a new record high. A pandemic would disrupt this financial bonanza: preventing people from traveling could spell financial disaster.

Disinformation—Trump Style

Meanwhile, in the U.S., the arrival of Covid-19 led to a disinformation campaign of another kind. This one was not based on a government's intentional efforts to try and preserve an economy affecting millions of people, but rather on the actions of a misguided political leader—Donald Trump. To fully understand the behavior of President Trump during the pandemic, you need first to have a peripheral knowledge of his personality. A short detour into this is presented here. This is an important background to understanding his disinformation campaign.

Politics, Power, and the Personality of an Autocrat

Donald J. Trump began his career in real estate after graduating from the University of Pennsylvania's Wharton School of Finance and Commerce in 1968. He worked for his father's real estate business and eventually took it over in 1971.

In the early 1990s, following an economic downturn and slump in the real estate market, Trump was deeply in debt; several of his casinos filed for bankruptcy. In 1995, he reported nearly $1 billion loss on his taxes. Although he declared many bankruptcies, believing in himself and projecting confidence, he was successful in convincing lenders that he could do better and secured more loans. He eventually made a financial comeback, in part with a business model that involved licensing his name for a wide variety of ventures ranging from condominiums to steaks and neckties. He continued to acquire and develop real estate properties. Years of thinking himself right and yet not accomplishing everything he wanted instilled in him a strong desire to get things done in his own way. Producing and starring in his own reality television show, *The Apprentice,* between 2003 and 2015 was one way he attempted that. Becoming the president of the United States gave him even more power and the means to do just that on a much larger scale.

He got into presidential politics believing that the country was becoming too focused on the needs of other countries in the world, with less emphasis on the interests of the USA. He felt that the political system and the way Congress worked needed to be changed and he believed that the only way to accomplish this was by having someone like him take charge of making the changes that he felt were long overdue.

The 2016 presidential race was very divisive, in part due to a number of inflammatory remarks and tweets made by Trump. He was convinced that his projection of confidence, rather than reasoning based on evidence, was the critical component in achieving his goal. While some members of the Republican establishment distanced themselves from the candidate, Trump's supporters admired his outspokenness and perceived business success, along with the fact that he wasn't a politician. As a result, he won in a surprising victory over Hillary Clinton.

However, he soon found out that in a democratic political system, governing requires more than the projection of confidence that got him elected. He was expected to answer probing questions not only about the value of achieving his desired goals, which some people disagreed with, but also the rationale and methodology to be used. Having no patience, inclination to work, or training to learn the details sufficient to answer the questions truthfully, he ignored those "irritations" and resorted to his proven tactic of simply appealing directly to his millions of followers using social media, especially Twitter.

In this regard, he seems to have copied Hitler's playbook. Instead of talking down to people as politicians before him did, Hitler talked *to* them. Similarly, Trump made his followers believe that he was one of them and that he loved them. They were ready to believe what he said and did, without questioning his motives, his methods, or whether his results actually benefitted them.

To keep the millions of followers interested in his promises and motivated to be loyal to him, he used two prominent emotional motivators—anger and fear—much as how Hitler used these emotions in Germany to appeal to the populace. Trump knew that in times of hardship, people will always look for scapegoats to blame, and even to hate.

To accomplish his goal of doing everything his own way, Trump made all major policy decisions himself and selected people who would carry out his decisions without dissent. He regularly terminated anyone who did not faithfully follow his plan. For example, here is a partial list of people who were either terminated or who voluntarily departed after starting their job in the Trump Administration.

> Attorney General William P. Barr*; Secretary of Defense Mark T. Esper*; Director of Cyber Security and Infrastructure Security Agency Christopher Krebs*; Inspector General (Intelligence) Michael Atkinson*; Ambassador to the European Union Gordon Sondland*; Navy Secretary Richard V. Spencer*; Energy Secretary Rick Perry*; Dep. Director of National Intelligence Sue Gordon*; Russian Ambassador John Huntsman*; Secretary of Labor Alex Acosta*; Customs and Border Protection Commissioner (acting) John Sanders*; Chairwoman of CPSC (acting) Ann Marie Buerkle*; Chairman of Council of Economic Advisers Kevin Hassett*; Director of U.S. Citizenship and

Immigration Services L. Francis Cissna*; Secretary of Homeland Security Kristjen Nieson*; Secret Service Director Randolph "Tex" Alles; SBA Administrator Linda McMahon*; Air Force Secretary Heather Wilson*; FDA Commissioner Scott Gottlieb*; Dep. Attorney General Rod Rosenstein*; FEMA Administrator Brock Long*; Secretary of Defense Jim Mattis*; Interior Secretary Ryan Zinke*; Chief of Staff John Kelly; Department of National Security Advisor Mira Ricardel; Attorney General Jeff Sessions*; U.N Ambassador Nikki Haley*; Director of Office of Personnel Management Jeff Pon*; White House Counsel Donald McGahn; White House Legislative Affairs Director Marc Short; Environmental Protection Agency Administrator Scott Pruitt*; Secretary of Veterans Affairs David Shulkin*; and Secretary of State Rex Tillerson* [* Represents cabinet and other positions requiring Senate confirmation]

It is well understood that democracy can only be successful when groups with strong views on any subject compromise for the common good. It is also critically important in democracy that there be a free press to report to the general public the points of view of opposing sides as the reporting of facts, not opinions, and to clearly clarify any personal beliefs of a journalist in the matter being discussed.

Trump conducted his presidency to take advantage of the emotional resentment of (mostly white) Americans who believed that the government was wasting their money, especially on social programs for immigrants from Latin America who were crossing the border to escape poverty and political chaos in their own countries. Over time, many sub-groups of Americans felt marginalized because of what they perceived as too many compromises that they were forced to tolerate as normal. When Trump came along and, like Hitler, suggested that what they thought was to be tolerated was in fact something he could easily change, they began to have hope.

For example, hearing, repeatedly, the (distorted) message of creeping socialism and "Antifa" mobs burning cities, many Americans felt that they were losing what they considered as their fundamental right to a peaceful life and lawful pursuit of happiness. This created a viral kind of anger. People began to believe that Trump was the leader who could correct all the wrongs, regardless of any truth about these wrongs. He was able to convince enough voters that the "elites" were trying to manipulate and control ordinary Americans to fit their self-serving ideologies. He put the blame on the "biased" news media as the real culprit, not for failing to explain the facts but as purveyors of "fake" news.

When reporters asked for clarification for such characterizations or about the real facts, they were subjected to hostility, personal insults, and branded as "enemy of the people." Trump even took actions to reduce funding for news organizations such as PBS and tried to attack the owners of the Washington Post and CNN for being against his interests and therefore against the interests of the American people.

In short, he acted as an extremely competent and confident captain who used the wind to blow the ship in the desired direction. However, unlike a ship's captain, Trump also sought to increase the force of anxiety-related winds, often seeking to disturb societal peace with wild and false accusations, divisive comments on Twitter, racial and otherwise, and self-serving statements that blamed others for causing or not solving the country's problems. Trump supporters accepted everything he said without question and hailed him as a great leader.

In addition, a segment of the press was always eager to talk and write about Trump supporters' most ignorant prejudices as if they were opinions that deserved expression, using the rationale that this is what the supporters wanted from the press. In effect, this created a closed loop of self-serving prejudices and falsehoods.

Once Trump started accumulating more and more followers, often referred to as his "base," he was successful at keeping his opponents silent by creating a fear of retribution from his growing group of supporters. Republican members of Congress were intimidated into never contradicting or questioning Trump; they knew that a negative tweet from him would quickly taint their reputation. Worse, they also knew that his lambasts against them would be immediately amplified by multiple programs in the conservative news media, especially Fox News. For example, throughout his presidential term, whenever a GOP Senator or House member raised concerns, he or she faced Trump's social media wrath followed by angry calls from Republican party members and primary challenges from newcomers who pledged loyalty to Trump. The power of his hold on the rank and file of the Republican Party was evident by the way Republican officials at many levels of the government not only failed to stand up to his many authoritarian demands but were convinced of his views and facilitated their implementation.

How Trump Misled the U.S. about Covid-19

Covid-19 was not a medical or scientific problem for Trump, but a political game perfectly suited to his character that allowed him to follow through on his 2016 campaign claim, "I alone can fix it." As soon as he was made aware of Covid-19, he believed that it was the perfect situation to give him an excellent chance to prove himself. However, not having the patience to think through the problem or to formulate a plan of action, he relied on what he knew best: getting his information from sources such as Fox News rather than scientists and using his social media communication skills to project an image of competence. He was confident that he would lead America through the pandemic; that confidence was based solely on his messaging capabilities.

To accomplish this objective, he relied on extensive and constant disinformation about the origin, spread, and severity of the virus. He exaggerated claims or openly released false information about every issue of importance to the American public regarding how to stay alive and protect one's family and business from the virus: the use of masks, social distancing, virus therapies, testing availability, and incidence and death statistics. His false statements were regularly amplified by some members of the Trump family, cabinet secretaries,

Republicans in Congress, as well as thousands of local Republican community leaders and numerous key media personalities.

For months on end throughout 2020, the spread of coronavirus across the U.S. was in part facilitated by the false claims of President Trump, who desperately wanted to create the impression that he had taken a sound intellectual interest in and assumed authority over the medical science of the pandemic. As he later admitted, he deliberately downplayed the seriousness of the virus, at first comparing it to the seasonal flu and later blaming the media for creating the "hysteria." He predicted the virus would "magically" disappear and he belittled the statistics on infection cases and mortality.

Perhaps he sought to prevent panic among people and keep the economy strong. But if this was his goal, he completely ignored what would have been the most logical advice about virus containment strategies such as aggressive testing, isolation of infected individuals, surveillance, contact tracing, and quarantine of exposed individuals along with mitigation measures such as mask mandates, physical distancing, and avoidance of crowded places. If Trump did anything of value as a leader throughout 2020, it was that he aggressively pushed for vaccine development. Unfortunately, he had no authority over the coronavirus.

The Early Spread of the Covid-19 Pandemic

The first National Security Council meeting on the new illness spreading in China was on January 14, 2020. Health officials could not answer basic questions due to the lack of information from the ground because the U. S government could not get permission to send personnel from the Centers for Disease Control and Prevention to Wuhan.

On January 15, 2020, Trump hosted the Chinese delegation in the East Room for signing a trade deal. The Chinese representatives didn't say a word about the virus. On January 27, Deputy national security adviser Matthew Pottinger called a cabinet-level meeting attended by the top one or two officials from the relevant agencies: Health and Human Services Secretary Alex Azar, CDC Director Robert Redfield, Deputy Secretary of State Stephen Biegub, and National Institute of Allergy and Infectious Disease Director Dr. Anthony S. Fauci. Those in attendance at that meeting discussed what Pottinger had heard from a very high-level doctor in China: the new virus was expected to be worse than SARS in 2003 and more like the influenza pandemic of 1918 that killed an estimated 50 million people worldwide. Pottinger was also aware of the potential for asymptomatic spread of Covid-19.

On Tuesday, January 28th, he briefed Trump in the Oval Office. He recommended that the president immediately ban travel from China. However, Dr. Fauci was not convinced of the need for a travel ban until January 30th when the first U.S. case of human-to-human transmission was confirmed. On January 31st , Trump announced the travel ban to and from China.

Chinese authorities immediately complained that certain countries were creating tensions that could lead to panic. They allowed continued travel to and from China to other countries, thus aiding the spread of the pandemic. Although the Chinese Communist Party's (CCP) lack of truthfulness and transparency were known, which should have caused suspicion and doubt in the U.S., many top U. S. administration officials, concerned about the economy, insisted that the national security team was overreacting and the media was exaggerating the threat in an effort to bring down Trump.

On February 6th, after a lengthy conversation with the President of China, Xi Jinping, the White House issued a statement saying, "President Trump expressed confidence in China's strength and resilience in confronting the challenge of the 2019 novel coronavirus outbreak." It suggested that President Trump was led to believe that the virus was not a threat to people outside China and most likely would go away when the weather got warmer. Trump repeated that reassuring message to the American public on February 10, 2020.

As the coronavirus spread across the globe in February 2020, the World Health Organization urged avoidance of terms like the

"Wuhan virus" or the "Chinese virus," fearing it could create anger against Asians. Yet, on March 16, 2020, as the pandemic began to spread across the U.S., Trump used a black sharpie to replace the term "Coronavirus" with "China virus" on the paper copy of a speech he was giving. His objective appeared to be to avoid taking any blame for the pandemic by redirecting the public's fears and anger towards China. Researchers later confirmed that after Trump mentioned "Chinese virus" in his tweet on March 16th, there were ten times the number of tweets using the hashtag *#chinesevirus* compared to the term #covid-19, which had been the dominant term prior to the President's March 16 tweet.

In May 2020, according to Bloomberg News, Secretary of State Michael Pompeo stated that "enormous evidence" showed the Covid-19 outbreak began in a laboratory in the central Chinese city of Wuhan. However, he provided no evidence to support that claim, nor did he clarify how the Trump administration was choosing to deal with the rapidly spreading viral infection in the U. S. Although knowing whether the virus came from the Wuhan laboratory might be extremely important to formulate security protocols at such facilities worldwide to prevent future viral pandemics, at the time this statement could be misinterpreted by Trump's followers as meaning that the blame belonged with the Chinese government.

The cumulative effects of Trump's disinformation campaign about the pandemic were evident in a June 2020 survey of over 1400 adult Americans representative of the U.S. population. The results indicated that, on average, 47% of conservatives selected Chinese Americans from a list of ethnic groups as those responsible for the pandemic. In addition, on a scale from 0 to 10, 10 being most severe, conservatives rated the severity of the virus as only 5.9 compared to moderates and liberals who rated it at 7.7. The net effect was, according to a report from the organization Stop AAPI Hate that was referenced in *The Washington Post* on March 19, 2021, there had been, at that time, nearly 3,800 anti-Asian American incidents in the U.S. since the epidemic began.[4]

The Story of the Wuhan Institute of Virology (WIV)

Most viral pandemics emerge when the virus passes from an animal to a human through "zoonotic" infection. Experts in virology determined that Covid-19 almost certainly was not engineered in a laboratory because it has several naturally occurring features and is closely related to a 2014 coronavirus that came from a bat in a cave in China.

But they also agreed they could not rule out that the virus may have escaped from the Wuhan Institute of Virology (WIV), a research lab that was studying coronaviruses to understand how viruses found in animals can infect humans. U.S officials had raised concerns about the safety protocols at WIV in 2018. "Whether the staff are interacting with bats in the wild or in the lab, they are routinely putting themselves at risk of infection," according to one unnamed U.S. scientist. While it is an extremely rare occurrence for an accidental human infection to happen during research done on viruses at a top level laboratory, plenty of virologists still argue that this was the likely path for the novel coronavirus, because no one had yet identified the animal that might have spread the virus to humans.

The WIV's predecessor, the Wuhan Microbiology Laboratory, was established in 1956 to study agricultural viruses and environmental research. After undergoing several changes in administration, as well as in names, the research institute became the Wuhan Institute of Virology in 1978. In the 1980s and 1990s, the WIV conducted award-winning studies in insect and animal viruses, on the molecular nature of viruses, and on virus classification and other microbes. In 2002, it was formally approved as a high-tech base-type research and development institute. The emergence of SARS in 2003 gave the lab an opportunity to study methods of control and prevention of emerging diseases. It was certified as a WHO reference laboratory.

Emerging Infectious Diseases [EID] are major threats to public health around the world. More than 70% originate from or are transmitted by wildlife such as a bat or a bird. By studying wildlife viruses, we can often uncover the animal origin and methods of transmission of human viruses, sequencing the genetic evolutions that enable the virus to jump from one animal to another and then to humans, and to formulate effective control methods. After SARS and Ebola epidemics, the WIV started studying these viruses.

On December 30, 2019, the Wuhan Municipal Health Commission issued an "urgent notice" to medical institutions in Wuhan saying that cases of pneumonia of unknown cause had emerged from the city's Huanan Seafood Wholesale market.

On February 3, 2020, WIV researchers reported in the journal *Nature* that the novel coronavirus spreading around the world was a bat-derived coronavirus. On February 6th, Botao Xiao, a molecular biomechanics researcher at South China University of Technology, posted a paper stating that the "killer coronavirus probably originated from a laboratory in Wuhan." He later withdrew the paper after Chinese authorities disputed his claim. There were two laboratories studying bats and coronaviruses located about 12 kilometers from the seafood market. Tissue samples and contaminated trash from these could have been the source of the pandemic.

In order to fully understand the origins of Covid-19, we need to get answers to the following questions:

1. It is known that the Wuhan Institute for Virology had mapped the virus genome by January 2, 2020 and had determined it to be a SARS-like coronavirus. What was the reason for the laboratory to be mapping the virus? Where did the sample come from? Who was in charge and how well was it supervised?
2. The Chinese government installed a military virologist to oversee the lab and the institute was ordered to destroy its samples and not to share them with U. S. researchers. Why was it necessary to put the military in charge of a research lab? Why were they told not to share any information with the United States?
3. On January 5, 2020, the Shanghai Public Health Clinical Center informed Chinese authorities that it also had identified and mapped the genome of the new virus. The lab was shut down the next day, after it released the report on the genome publicly. What was the reason for shutting down this laboratory; specifically, were there safety concerns?
4. *The Wall Street Journal* reported in May 2021 that a previously undisclosed U.S. intelligence report had found that three researchers from the lab who were conducting controversial research on the coronavirus were hospitalized with symptoms consistent with Covid-19 as early as November 2019, before the virus began spreading in China. It is noteworthy that the city of Wuhan is not known to have bats carrying coronavirus. It is imperative that the Chinese government release the full medical information about the nature of those researchers' illnesses and the treatments they received.

The Further Consequences of Trump's Disinformation

Through the second half of 2020, President Trump continued to dish out more falsehoods and unscientific claims about the pandemic. In July 2020, his administration delivered a strong argument for school reopenings in the autumn without commenting on health risks to children or the adults working with them. A suggestion Trump issued in August discouraged the testing of people without Covid-19 symptoms even when they had contact with infected individuals. It was later learned that Trump believed that more testing would yield more positive infection results, making him look bad in the media.

Continuing the same narrative, on October 30, 2020, Donald Trump, Jr. declared on *Fox News* that Covid-19 deaths were ``almost nothing"—on a day that the virus killed 1,004 Americans. For the next six months, the deaths due to coronavirus infection climbed and climbed, reaching, on an average, over 2,400 per day during the first ten days of December 2020.

All during this time, Trump appeared to have been adept at exploiting the need for people to have certainty when faced with a pandemic caused by an unknown agent. He was able to blame the uneven and chaotic response to the outbreak once it began spreading within the United States on the failure of state governments to act. Meanwhile, science had to wait for the collection of data and analysis before issuing guidelines and methods of implementation to contain the pandemic.

How Disinformation Resonated Beyond Trump

Trump tried different approaches to drive home his belief in the insignificance of the pandemic's severity that nearly all health experts were highly alarmed about. By assessing the response of his followers to his original disinformation and finding that some people in the media were repeating his suggestions and commenting on them positively, he characterized this as an affirmation of his original idea to make the virus a non-issue in terms of the health and well-being of the American people. Trump's pattern of communication, using art and entertainment for message amplification through social media—a novel cultural phenomenon—attracted even larger audiences who equally did not want to believe the science that indicated that the virus was extremely deadly.

Trump's behavior based on his belief that his followers accepted his ideas and that their numbers were growing raised concerns among those around him in the White House. For example, as the number of coronavirus cases increased in November 2020, and with concerns about families congregating for Thanksgiving, four doctors on President Trump's coronavirus task force—Dr. Deborah Birx, Dr. Anthony Fauci, Dr. Stephen Hahn, and Dr. Robert Redfield—warned senior administration officials about the need for dramatic action to slow the spread. They wanted the president to be proactive in promoting the wearing of face masks and for the administration to dramatically expand testing. However, White House Chief of Staff Mark Meadows, emboldened by Trump, told the doctors that he did not believe their troubling data assessment. Likewise, Vice President Mike Pence, who was aware of the recommendations of these doctors, also ignored their warning.

Let's look at some of the areas in which Trump amplified his disinformation:

Trump's Disinformation about Masks

In the early days of the pandemic, Trump disagreed with the idea of federal mandates to reduce the spread of the virus, most specifically with the idea of making it a national requirement to wear masks in public places. He announced that wearing a mask was voluntary and that he would not wear one. He frequently appeared during coronavirus task force briefings without a mask. He refused to speak out or even model healthy behavior patterns such as wearing a face mask, which would have saved tens of thousands of lives, in spite of recommendations from his own advisory panel. He repeatedly cast doubt about their efficacy and brazenly demonstrated his doubt about the usefulness of wearing one when he publicly removed his mask upon returning to the White House after his hospital stay to be treated for the virus. It is possible that he relied on reports such as the one which was published online at Annals.org on April 6, 2020 (Bae S, Kim MC, Kim JY, et al. Effectiveness of surgical and cotton masks in blocking SARS-CoV-2: a controlled comparison in 4 patients.) However, it should be pointed out that the authors of that report retracted the article after recognizing the concept of limit of detection (LOD) of the in-house reverse transcriptase polymerase chain reaction used in the study. Trump continued to show his disdain for mask wearing throughout nearly all of 2020, regardless of his own bout with the virus in early October of that year.

Dr. Robert Redfield, director of the CDC, testified before the Senate in September 2020 that masks are "the most important, powerful public health tool we have" for containing the pandemic. Yet, Trump maintained that wearing a mask in the Oval Office was not for him, and he refused to wear one even when greeting world leaders. He suggested it was a recommendation from the CDC (Centers for Disease Control and Prevention) that he would not be following. He even claimed in October 2020 that 85% of people diagnosed with Covid-19 wore masks—a complete mischaracterization of a CDC study. (The CDC study compared two groups of people who had tested positive and negative for the coronavirus and found that a much higher percentage of the positive cases had had close contact with someone known to have Covid-19. In the 14 days before they got sick, according to the study, 71 percent of people who tested positive and 74 percent of people who tested negative reported "always" wearing a mask in public.[5]

Masks and Aerosol Transmission

To fully understand the role of masks and social distancing in containing the spread of Covid-19 it helps to understand how the virus spreads. Droplet transmission is the most common mode of Covid-19 transmission. This happens when respiratory droplets generated by coughing, sneezing, or talking come in contact with mucosal surfaces of the nose, eyes, and mouth. Transmission can also occur indirectly via contact with hands on contaminated surfaces and then touching mucosal surfaces on the body. These droplet particles are large and are not able to remain suspended in the air for long periods of time and so are usually dispersed over short distances. The size of the particles for droplet infections is greater than 5 µm. ("µm" is the scientific symbol for micrometer, a micrometer being one millionth of a meter.) Covid-19 also spreads through even smaller-sized droplets called aerosols that can stay suspended in the air longer and move with air currents.

A significant feature of viral pandemics is the ability of the virus to mutate within human beings, as mentioned earlier. For example the original version of the coronavirus that came out of China mutated to create what is known as the UK variant that was found to be more transmissible but not necessarily more virulent, according to some studies. Later we became aware of Brazilian and South African variants of Covid-19. One of these mutations allowed the virus to spread more efficiently and the other allowed it to evade the immune system. In mid-2021, the Indian variant began spreading globally, containing features of both UK and Brazilian mutations in the same strain of the coronavirus. Called the Delta variant, it is more contagious and transmissible and by the summer of 2021, it became the dominant strain of the coronavirus throughout much of the world.

Covid-19 can be easily transmitted in confined spaces where people breathe the same air containing viruses. It is clear that under these circumstances, masks work to reduce the rate of transmission. In fact, according to some, it is likely that masks have been used to prevent respiratory transmission of infectious illnesses in healthcare settings since the Middle Ages.

A Chinese-Malaysian doctor named Wu Lien-teh is credited with popularizing masks fashioned from gauze bandages and wool to protect himself and his team during the deadly Manchurian plague in the early 1900s. In early 2020, the U.S. Health and Human Services proposed to send free masks to every American household. a step that some public health experts think would have depoliticized mask-wearing. However, senior White House officials believed that this step would unnecessarily alarm people, unhelpfully comparing it to wearing "underwear on your face."

Due to the lack of a centrally coordinated Federal directive, state and local responses varied widely on mask wearing. Some states continued to maintain no mask directives, allowing businesses to set their own rules.

Trump's Disinformation about Social Distancing

Unlike the relatively easy transmissibility of the virus when people are indoors, being outdoors reduces transmissibility immensely. Even when passing others at close distance, it is incredibly unlikely that one can catch the virus. Although not impossible, researchers have yet to identify proven cases of such transmission through encounters with others for a second or two while being outdoors.

A study co-authored by Stanford engineering researchers showed that the coronavirus has spread faster in America's jails and prisons than it did in Wuhan, China during the pandemic's outbreak.[6] The primary reason, according to the researchers, is that there is very little opportunity for social distancing in prisons. It's common to have two or more people per cell and sanitary conditions are comparatively low. Cook County Jail in Illinois had one of the largest outbreaks in the country, and the infection rate at Rikers Island was nearly five times that of New York City.

On February 25, 2020, Nancy Messonier, director of the National Center for Immunization and Respiratory Diseases, warned that it was not a question of whether there would be pandemic but when. Mr. Trump was so enraged with the statement that the agency was prevented from spreading the warning. The White House began to require the CDC guideline documents regarding social distancing in church choirs, bars, and restaurants to be revised; the administration also prevented the CDC from conducting regular news conferences, compared to 13 news conferences in one month during the West Africa Ebola outbreak six years previously.

It is noteworthy that even though systems to alert people of the spread of infectious diseases did not exist in 1918, during the flu pandemic of that year actions were taken to impose maritime quarantines on islands such as Iceland, Australia, and American Samoa and social distancing measures were introduced by closing schools, theaters, and places of worship, limiting public transportation, and banning mass gatherings. A later study found that measures such as banning mass gatherings and requiring the wearing of face masks could cut the death rate up to 50%, depending on how soon they were imposed and provided they were not lifted prematurely. [7]

On February 26, 2020, the first case of asymptomatic community spread was reported in the U.S. Yet, on February 29th, CDC director Robert Redfield said at a White House press briefing: "The American public needs to go on with their normal life. Okay? We are continuing to aggressively investigate these new community links . . . . But at this stage, again, the risk is low." A later report from researchers at the University of Notre Dame was in line with his reasoning; that report claimed to have found only 1,514 cases by early March, when in fact more than 100,000 people were already infected.[8]

Trump's attempts to minimize the threat posed by the virus, his continuing focus on the economy, his impeachment, and his holding of his own political gatherings are all easy to understand in light of his personality. When he showed frustration with those around him who began panicking, he had them modify their messaging regarding the virus. Health and Human Services Secretary Alex Azar briefed White House reporters in February 2020, saying, "the risk of infection for American people remains low." A few days later, National Security Advisor Robert O'Brien, appearing on CBS's "Face the Nation," said, "This is something that is a low risk, we think, in the U.S."

Through this messaging, the president's disinformation strategy seriously minimized the virus threat, perhaps in an effort to create the impression that he was fully capable of taking the necessary initiatives to control the pandemic. However, by pretending to assume authority over medical science, Trump set the absolute wrong tone and prevented others within his administration from telling the truth about the virus, despite being well aware of the true nature of the risk. No one was allowed to contradict Trump publicly, and thus the government's official policy on the pandemic was driven by Trump's ego.

What the president may not have realized is that in science, truth is what is presented at the time based on the interpretation of available evidence. That truth must be amenable to change as new evidence or reinterpretation of old evidence appear. For example, both Dr. Fauci and Dr. Redfield, when presented with new evidence, changed their assessment of the spread of coronavirus and started advocating social distancing, hand washing, and using face masks, not only to protect oneself but also to protect others.

However, despite having a golden opportunity to show leadership by not only obtaining more information about the behavior of the new virus directly from Chinese officials and acting more decisively to contain the virus, Trump chose to minimize the threat posed by the novel coronavirus. He publicly disagreed with both Dr. Fauci and Dr. Redfield with regards to the importance of asymptomatic spread and proceeded to conduct political rallies without enforcing social distancing, both outdoors and indoors. He also regularly endorsed those who resented wearing face masks to protest what they termed was an infringement of their civil liberties. Some justified not wearing face masks as a way of showing their trust in God rather than in face masks.

The result of Trump's disinformation campaigns about Covid-19 is evidenced by the fact that by early September 2020, the U. S. accounted for 23% of all coronavirus cases and 21% of the deaths in the world, despite having only 4% of the world's population. Nearly 200,000 Americans had already died due to the virus and epidemiologists projected a rise in cases and fatalities in the late fall and winter as cold weather would send people indoors, students would return to schools and colleges, and the pandemic would converge with flu season.

By comparison, during a similar period of time, the nation of Taiwan, with its 24 million people, situated less than 100 miles off the coast of mainland China, had only 449 confirmed cases of Covid-19 and seven deaths. This result was obtained because scientists in Taiwan recommended and government officials agreed to put into effect, with the cooperation of the general public, the following: regular use of face masks, social distancing of at least six feet between non-family members, frequent hand washing, testing early and often to identify infected persons, isolation until proven not contagious, rigorous contact tracing, and quarantining of exposed people for at least two weeks.

Similarly, by mid-September, Europe had reported 4.4 million cases and 217,278 deaths among a population of 750 million, while the U.S. reported 6.7 million cases and 198,000 deaths in a population less than half of Europe's, 330 million. These tragic discrepancies need to be placed where the fault belongs—at the feet of Donald Trump. His repeated attempts to downplay the pandemic lured a good part of the population into a false sense of security. The effect of ignoring public health guidelines such as facial coverings and social distancing, combined with colder weather that increased indoor gatherings, was evident by September 2020 when the dramatic rise in infections was clearly seen.

Trump's Disinformation about Testing

During a pandemic, diagnostic testing is vital for finding out who is infected so that the patient can be isolated and contacts identified before the contagion spreads more widely. Testing at any given time can potentially reduce the risk of Covid-19 transmission by 37% to 61%, based on mathematical modelling by the CDC. The deaths of 39 inmates at the Life Care Center of Kirkland, Washington in early 2020 should have alerted the CDC and public health officials that testing was absolutely necessary to isolate infected individuals.

In the early days of the pandemic, it soon became clear that nursing homes lacked sufficient testing kits. Although they isolated the residents with symptoms, asymptomatic residents and staff moved in and out, spreading the virus. For example, when Morgan Katz of Johns Hopkins University School of Medicine checked Baltimore nursing homes, she found more than 38% of its residents tested positive.

On January 13, 2020, the World Health Organization made public a recipe for how to configure a test to detect the spreading viral threat of Covid-19. South Korea used testing to rapidly trace and contain outbreaks, keeping its overall disease and death rates low. But in the United States, scientists had trouble with every aspect of testing: developing a reliable test, ramping up test kit production, finding adequate chemical reagents for the kits, planning for an adequate number of testing sites, and conducting testing in a timely fashion. Although Trump announced a grand plan for drive-through test sites at CVS, Target, Walmart, and Walgreen parking lots, in the end, only 78 sites materialized nationwide.

Trump's attitude towards testing was completely incoherent and anti-scientific. During a political rally in June 2020, Trump stated the following: "When you do testing to that extent, you're going to find more people, you're going to find more cases. So I said to my people, 'Slow the testing down, please.' They test and they test." Slowing the testing was the opposite of what the nation needed.

The Story of Covid-19 Testing in the United States

The traditional efforts such as testing, isolation of the sick, and contact tracing can be a challenge under ordinary circumstances, but it can be a daunting challenge when a virus spreads at an exponential rate, even without a disinformation campaign such as the one conducted by Trump and propagated by his followers.

In the first week in January, Nancy Messonnier, director of the CDC's National Center for Immunization and Respiratory Diseases, asked Stephen Lindstrom, an accomplished virus specialist, how soon he could fashion a coronavirus test kit. On January 9th, Lindstrom outlined his plans for developing a test based on PCR, a multi-step test to detect viruses in humans using a sample of sputum or other genetic material. A machine would extract nucleic acids from the sample, copy and amplify targeted regions of the coronavirus genome, and identify the virus.

By the third week in January 2020, Thailand, Japan, South Korea, and Taiwan were all using molecular testing based on the virus's genetic sequence made public by the Chinese. The CDC said that they were focusing on a more sophisticated test, sensitive enough to detect close variants of the virus. Meanwhile, 120 public health labs were without a CDC-approved test.

Lindstrom saw no trouble with his test when he confirmed the diagnosis of the first U.S. patient on January 19.

On February 4th, he obtained emergency authorization from the FDA for the use of his test. However, soon state labs were claiming unacceptable levels of false-positive results. The CDC halted shipments of the test kits until after removal of a troublesome ingredient in it. On February 26th, almost a month and a half after the World Health Organization publicly shared its protocol for coronavirus testing, the FDA told the CDC that public health labs could use the test that was now devoid of the troublesome ingredient.

Taiwan, which started testing for coronavirus in January, had experienced death rates less than 2 per 100,000 people. In the United States, the rate was 91 deaths per 100,000 in the same time period. Brett Giroir, who served as the nation's coronavirus testing czar, referencing the administration's repeated claims in March 2020 that anyone who sought a coronavirus test could get one, clarified the truth on CNN in 2021 when he said, "There were components of the test available, but not the full meal deal."

On August 20, 2020, the Trump administration blocked the Food and Drug Administration from regulating a broad swath of laboratory tests, including for the coronavirus, in a move strongly opposed by the agency. The new policy stunned many health experts and laboratories because of its timing, several months into a pandemic. Some public health experts warned that the shift could result in unreliable coronavirus tests on the market, potentially worsening the testing crisis that had dogged the U.S. They argued the change was unlikely to solve current testing problems, which at this point were largely due to shortages of supplies such as swabs and chemical reagents.

But supporters cheered the change as long overdue, saying it could help get new and more innovative tests to market more quickly. They said that the FDA review process sharply slowed testing at the beginning of the pandemic and that the new policy could ensure such bottlenecks don't recur.

Trump's coronavirus task force was equally handicapped, unable to do what needed to be done to gain control over coronavirus infection rates and deaths. Both Dr. Anthony Fauci and Dr. Deborah Birx stated in 2021—after Trump was defeated in the election and they felt they could finally tell the truth—that Trump refused to allow them to take a scientific approach to the pandemic. "I was marginalized every day. I mean, that is no question. The majority of the people in the White House did not take this seriously," said Birx.

Trump's Disinformation about Treatments for Covid-19

Nowhere in handling the Covid-19 pandemic is Trump's disinformation strategy more evident than his obsession with providing unscientific and outright false information on Covid-19 treatments.

At first, early in the pandemic, when many patients were severely ill with fever, cough, and respiratory distress, there was as yet no specific treatment for the virus other than symptomatic and supportive care. President Trump, on January 22, 2020, claimed, "We do have a plan." On February 23rd, he insisted, "We have it very much under control in this country." On March 10th he said, "Just stay calm. It will go away." During all this time, in fact, Trump, for all practical purposes, had no plan to treat Covid-19, and was openly defying his own medical experts.

It is true that, when faced with an unknown infectious agent, people sometimes become desperate and try unproven and even dangerous treatments. Sometimes even doctors try medications not approved for a specific infection, as long as it was approved for use in another illness, thinking that it may not do much harm. This was the case with hydroxychloroquine, a drug that was safe and effective for use in patients with autoimmune disease or malaria, when it was tested for use in the prevention and/or treatment for Covid-19. The testing was conducted in a nonrandomized study on 36 patients with documented Covid-19. Among 26 patients who received hydroxychloroquine, 6 stopped the treatment early. Among the 20 left at day 6 after treatment, 70% (14/20) were "virologically" cured, compared with 12.5% (2/16) in the control group. This small study suggested a possible benefit, and perhaps led to Trump's endorsement of hydroxychloroquine as a promising option to treat Covid-19. However, this test was insufficient to prove that hydroxychloroquine was responsible for the cured patients.

Top health officials in the Trump administration, including Drs. Fauci and Brix, agreed that that particular test among a small population did not prove hydroxychloroquine's effectiveness, and said that other clinical trials showed the drug to be unhelpful. In truth, the scientific community was somewhat divided on the drug in the beginning. On one hand, Ashish Jha, dean of Brown University School of Public Health, testified against use of the drug. On the other, Harvey Rish, a professor of epidemiology and public health at Yale University, supported its use. George Fareed, a family medicine specialist in Brawley, California testified that he had effectively treated Covid-19 patients with it, but he never produced a scientifically validated controlled study.

Nevertheless, Trump began promoting hydroxychloroquine as a sure cure for Covid-19, despite the lack of scientific evidence that proved it actually worked. Many in the medical community warned about the dangers of this drug for patients with underlying medical conditions. However, Trump's trade adviser Peter Navarro tried to pressure Rick Bright, the director of the Federal Biomedical Advanced Research and Development Authority, to stockpile hydroxychloroquine in the Strategic National Stockpile for distributing millions of doses, and in April 2020 the White House ordered the distribution of 23 million doses to a dozen states.

In addition, the Senate Homeland Security Committee under chairman Sen. Ron Johnson began holding hearings on hydroxychloroquine. Chairman Johnson, Republican senator from Wisconsin, criticized the medical community for, as he saw it, turning a blind eye on the drug simply because of Trump's promotion of it. But in the end, the FDA withdrew its emergency-use authorization for hydroxychloroquine in hospitalized patients because the safety risks—including heart problems—outweighed the potential benefits.

The Aftermath of Trump's Disinformation Campaigns

The evidence shows that President Trump repeatedly offered falsehoods about the coronavirus pandemic. His attempts at proving that he was in control of the pandemic turned out to be false, ignorant, and anti-scientific disinformation that served his own ego, but not the country.

The examples of his falsification of pandemic facts and statistics are abundant. These are just a few:

On Friday, February 7 and Wednesday, February 19, 2020, Trump claimed that the virus would soon just disappear. He stated, "When we get into April, in the warm weather, that has a very negative effect on [. . .] that type of a virus." On Thursday, February 27th, he said again, "It's going to disappear. One day, it's like a miracle—it will disappear." In May, he claimed that the "coronavirus numbers were looking much better, going down almost everywhere, cases are way down," when in fact, cases were either increasing or plateauing in the majority of U.S. states.

On Wednesday, June 17th, he claimed that the pandemic was "fading away. It is going to fade away." At this time, the country was still seeing 20,000 new cases daily. When the daily cases more than doubled to 50,000, on Thursday, July 12th he claimed the pandemic is "getting under control." On Saturday, July 4th he claimed "99% of Covid-19 cases are totally harmless." On Monday, July 6th he claimed, "We have the lowest fatality (mortality) rate in the world." The true case/fatality rate (the ratio of deaths to confirmed Covid-19 cases) was 4.1%, which placed the U.S. in the middle of global rankings.

Multiple times, he claimed that children are "very immune" to Covid-19. He also appeared in the news media multiple times to assure us that America is "rounding the corner" and "rounding the final turn." He made statements like this both before and after cases in the U.S. were known to be still rising in 47 of 50 states. He also pretended that testing was the problem: "Cases are going up in the U.S. because we are testing far more than any other country." The truth was actually that positive cases were outpacing tests around the country.

A set of guidelines about the country's reopening released in April 2020 by the White House was far less accurate than what had been drafted by the CDC and the Federal Emergency Management Agency. *The Washington Post* reported on April 9, 2021, that it was Trump's political appointees who had managed to rewrite any scientific reports from the CDC that they deemed unfavorable to Trump's message.

For example, after an outbreak of coronavirus at a Georgia summer camp, the CDC drafted a report with the opening line arguing for the need to understand youth transmission of coronavirus in order to develop guidelines for schools and institutes of higher education. But because of pressure from Trump political appointees, that language was changed to state that there was "limited data" about the spread of coronavirus among people under age 21.

Some Trump appointees believed that the President's goal was to stay focused on the economic cost of not reopening the country, because of the harm done to the economy during the national shutdowns. But in the final analysis, it appears that Trump's major concern was to preserve his standing as commander-in-chief and to appeal to his base of supporters who were themselves anti-maskers, anti-science, and anti-government. Appealing to them would, in Trump's mind, assure that he would be reelected, no matter how many infections and deaths the pandemic might cause.

Dr. Anthony Fauci, the chief medical adviser to President Joe Biden, said on CNN's *New Day* (Friday, January 22, 2021) that the lack of truthfulness from the Trump administration regarding the Covid-19 pandemic "very likely cost American lives, particularly when you're in the situation of almost being in a crisis with the number of cases and hospitalizations and deaths that we have—when you start talking about things that make no sense medically and no sense scientifically, that clearly is not helpful."

In March 2021, following a review, federal health officials at the CDC finally removed several controversial pandemic recommendations on the agency's website that were released during the Donald Trump administration. They were removed from the CDC website because they were "not primarily authored" by official staff at the CDC and thus did not reflect the best scientific evidence. During an interview presented by CNN in March 2021, Dr. Deborah Birx, a member of Trump's coronavirus task force, suggested that the vast majority of U.S. deaths due to Covid-19, after the first 100,000, could have been prevented if all Americans had followed guidelines regarding social distancing and gatherings. An analysis by Columbia University based on transmission rates between March 15 and May 2, 2020 concluded that if the country had shut down two weeks earlier, it could have prevented 82% of deaths and 84% of infections at that time.[9]

By the end of the summer of 2021, more than a year into the pandemic that had sickened tens of millions of people in the United States, over 600,000 Americans had died from the pandemic. Although as infection rates began dropping in the spring of 2021, federal health authorities had relaxed mask recommendations for people who are fully vaccinated against the virus, by August 2021, only about half the eligible people in the country had received at least one dose of coronavirus vaccines authorized for emergency use by the Food and Drug Administration.

As I write this chapter, it appears that we have turned into two nations—one of states with Democratic governors and/or left-leaning populations whose residents are mostly vaccinated and the other of Republican-leaning states whose populations have much lower vaccination rates, due in part to people refusing to be vaccinated. Few health officials can understand why millions of people in these Republican states are shunning the vaccines, which have proven to be far more effective against Covid-19 (and even the Delta variant) than originally thought. In July 2021, it was reported that 99.2% of all coronavirus-related deaths in Kentucky were people who were not vaccinated, and by September 2021, numerous states had higher death rates than when the pandemic first started, nearly all of which were among unvaccinated patients..

Once again, Trump has something to do with this massive vaccination failure in numerous Republican states. Despite having caught Covid-19, which caused his hospitalization for what is now believed to be a severe case, Trump continued to refuse to be a spokesperson for the vaccines. Although he and his family were vaccinated before he left the Oval Office in January 2021, he did not tell the American public that he received the vaccination, nor did he publicly state that he believes everyone should be vaccinated. One might hope that as he could begin to see the majority of Covid-related deaths occurring among the unvaccinated, he would send a different message. But the damage has already been done. At an appearance before a live audience in August 2021, he did tout vaccinations . . . and was booed by members of the audience. And his endorsement was half-hearted at best, as he also encouraged the crowd to continue believing they should "have their freedoms."

Such statements seem to represent intentional sabotage of the Biden administration's mostly successful efforts with vaccinations; perhaps Trump's motivation in that is retaliation based on his belief that President Biden is getting the credit for vaccinating the U.S. when it was Trump who pushed to get the vaccines developed and into the market with lightning speed. However, even in this regard, Trump would be relying on false premises. It is well known that the Trump administration, despite pushing for vaccine development, had no strategy to roll out the vaccines throughout the country. No plans had been made for how to vaccinate hundreds of millions of people before Trump left office. This is yet another example of Trump's inability to take any aspect of the pandemic seriously, using the only tools he knew how to use throughout the pandemic: falsehoods and intentional misstatements and prevarications, placing blame on others and taking credit that is not his to take. Unfortunately for the country, he was aided by those who not only supported him but also had the means to mislead others by misusing legitimate and technically accurate data.

The Resurgence of Covid-19 in Summer 2021

As this book is being finalized, the consequences of disinformation are once again becoming apparent in the deadly resurgence of the Delta variant of Covid-19. Yet disinformation still plagues us. Despite nearly 715,000 Covid-related deaths in the U.S. at this writing, predominantly among unvaccinated people, false information about the vaccine is still spreading rampantly on social media and such outlets as *Fox News*.

Chapter 1 Takeaways

- Disinformation has long plagued public health. Old time snake oil salesmen sold worthless cures to gullible people. This chapter highlights how disinformation became rampant about Covid-19, largely due to the efforts of President Donald Trump who ignored critical aspects of science-based public health guidelines. This is just one example of how disinformation from an influential source can cause the public to misunderstand the severity of a pandemic and suffer unnecessary health problems and even death. There is disinformation about many other diseases and health issues as well.

- Pandemics should actually be considered lifestyle diseases because they would not occur if people did not live a certain lifestyle that facilitates their spread. If one person gets a virus and does not leave their house, they are unlikely to spread the virus to others outside their home. The best evidence to support this notion that the novel coronavirus pandemic should be considered a lifestyle illness is the fact that the virus spread globally as humans traveled from place to place using all available transportation systems.
- While the Chinese government participated in promoting disinformation about the origins of the virus, former President Donald Trump believed that the pandemic was the perfect situation to prove himself as the only person who could fix the situation. However, not having the patience to think through the problem or to formulate a plan of action, he relied on what he knew best: getting his information from sources such as Fox News rather than scientists and using his social media communication skills to project an image of competence.
- Trump relied on extensive and constant disinformation about the origin, spread, and severity of the virus. He exaggerated claims or openly released false information about every issue of importance to the American public regarding how to stay alive and protect one's family and business from the virus: the use of masks, social distancing, virus therapies, vaccinations, testing, and incidence and death statistics. His false statements were regularly amplified by members of the Trump family, cabinet secretaries, Republicans in Congress, as well as thousands of local Republican community leaders and numerous key media personalities.

CHAPTER 2

MISINFORMATION ABOUT TYPE 2 DIABETES

MOST PEOPLE THINK that Type 2 diabetes is simply a state of elevated blood glucose, however, that is not the complete story. More importantly, it is not a hormonal disease as we have been led to believe. In actuality, Type 2 diabetes is a dangerous lifestyle condition that can be controlled through diet if people are educated about it.

The misinformation about Type 2 diabetes leads millions of people to neglect essential healthful diet advice and slide down a slippery slope into developing persistent high blood sugar and eventually diabetes, which they believe must be treated with drugs and insulin injections. Worse, despite these medical treatments, people with Type 2 diabetes still end up with severe complications, including kidney disease, loss of vision, amputations, heart attack, stroke, and premature death. Type 2 diabetes has become one of the leading causes of disability and early death—and it is largely preventable in most people.

To understand how Type 2 diabetes mistakenly came to be thought of as a hormonal disease having to do with insulin, and the resulting glucose control (gluco-centric) paradigm that has evolved to treat it as a disease, we need to start with a general understanding of diabetes;

we especially need clarity about the two kinds of diabetes, what have come to be called Type 1 and Type 2.

Diabetes in general is diagnosed based on having an elevation of one's blood glucose level. Blood glucose is sometimes called blood sugar, but the word "sugar" does not refer to the sugar you eat, such as the white sugar you put in your coffee or mix into the batter when you bake a cake. So not putting sugar in your coffee or not eating cake has nothing to do with whether you might develop high blood sugar.

What constitutes blood sugar is the amount of glucose in your blood. Glucose is the molecule released during the digestion of various types of carbohydrates, mostly present in grains, vegetables, and fruits. When you eat these foods, glucose is absorbed into the body following their digestion. Every cell in the body uses glucose for its energy, so you need glucose in your bloodstream to feed all your cells. I will go into more detail about blood glucose a bit further on in this book.

Understanding Type 1 Diabetes

The cells in your body are surrounded by blood that flows by them. When a cell needs fuel, it seeks a glucose molecule outside of it. But the cell cannot tell if there happens to be glucose outside. The glucose does not automatically enter the cell all the time. This probably evolved as a mechanism to ensure that cells are not flooded by glucose even when they don't need it.

So how does the cell know when there is glucose available? This is the role of insulin, a hormone produced in the "islet" cells of the pancreas to help regulate intake and usage of glucose.

After a meal, the elevation of blood glucose signals the pancreas to produce and release insulin to notify cells that glucose is on the way. Insulin molecules attach to a "receptor" on the wall of a cell, which then sends a signal to the cell nucleus. Within the nucleus, the gene in charge sends a message to send over a "transporter" that grabs a molecule of glucose from outside the cell and brings it to the cell's interior, where it serves as fuel to produce adenosine triphosphate (ATP), which is the actual energy blast that the cell uses to function.

It was discovered about a thousand years ago by an observant healer in India that ants were gathering around the urine on the ground after a child peed. This observation eventually led to the scientific discovery in the 1800s that some children are born with a dysfunctional pancreas that does not produce any insulin. The islet cells simply don't work. Without insulin, these children could not utilize the glucose in their blood and their cells could not produce enough energy to function properly. Such children died at a young age.

This disease was called diabetes or hyperglycemia (meaning high blood glucose). In the beginning, it was not called Type 1 because there was no other type yet identified.

After the discovery of insulin in 1921, it was also discovered that if these children were injected with the hormone insulin, they would survive. You can imagine why children without insulin suffered and died at a young age when cells could not generate enough energy to perform metabolic functions, and how dramatically their lives would be changed with the administration of insulin.

Understanding (the So-called) Type 2 Diabetes

With the understanding of the role of insulin in glucose metabolism, it became obvious how a child whose pancreas does not produce insulin could develop diabetes. The universally acclaimed success of insulin to improve the quality of life and increase the lifespan of children with diabetes helped clarify that there is a direct association between normal blood sugar and treatment with insulin.

But the next challenge to medical science was understanding why some people who did not have diabetes as children developed high blood sugar as adults. It seemed very logical to conclude that in these adults, insulin was somehow associated with their hyperglycemia. But even ten years after the discovery of insulin, it was unclear what insulin's role was in adult-onset diabetes.

Using laboratory tests, scientists discovered an oddity. Using samples taken from their blood after a meal, adults with hyperglycemia were found to have plenty of normally functioning insulin in their bloodstream. This meant that the pancreas was functioning correctly, producing plenty of insulin. So why were these adults developing high blood sugar?

In 1931, a Viennese medical professor, Dr. Wilhelm Falta, hypothesized that perhaps in adults with diabetes, the cells do not respond to the natural insulin, though he did not know how or why. Dr. Falta's notion of cellular unresponsiveness was just a hypothesis to explain elevated blood glucose level in adults. It suggested his awareness that adult onset diabetes must be different from what is seen in children. It also suggested that he did not know the exact reason for this blood glucose elevation in adult diabetic patients and that before accepting it as fact, it had to undergo validation.

However, in 1979, Dr. Ralph A. DeFronzo had no such reservation or interest in scientific accuracy as he latched onto Falta's theory about adult-onset diabetes. Along with Dr. Jordan D. Tobin and Dr. Reubin Andres, both in the Department of Medicine at Yale University School of Medicine, he not only endorsed the theory of cellular unresponsiveness to insulin but also vigorously promoted it.

They developed a diagnostic test called the "the glucose clamp technique," whereby subjects were infused with insulin and glucose at the same time. Then measurements were taken to determine how quickly the glucose dissipated in the body. From these experiments, DeFronzo claimed that adult-onset diabetes was caused by the impairment of three simultaneously ongoing processes:

1. defective insulin secretion by the pancreas,
2. an impairment of glucose uptake by tissues, especially muscles and liver cells, despite the presence of insulin, and
3. impaired suppression of glucose output from the liver in the presence of insulin.

This third point is based on the fact that, in liver cells, the presence of insulin is supposed to prevent the liver from producing more glucose and letting it into the bloodstream. This bodily mechanism likely derived from the need to avoid flooding the bloodstream with too much glucose after eating.

In essence, these researchers were concluding that adult-onset diabetes develops when just three types of cells—muscle, liver, and fat cells—start "resisting" the presence of insulin. The insulin is there outside the cell, but the cell does not recognize its signal or respond to it, and thus does not allow the glucose to enter inside. This leaves glucose building up in the bloodstream—hence high blood sugar. After a meal, the large amount of glucose produced in digestion is not fully absorbed by cells and the individual walks around with hyperglycemia on a regular basis.

So what is the problem with having hyperglycemia on a regular basis for adults? The problem is actually quite serious and expansive. For one thing, glucose molecules attach to different proteins in the body and can interfere with their function. (The commonly used laboratory test called "hemoglobin A1c" is an example of this attachment of glucose to the protein called hemoglobin.) Another problem with excess glucose absorption into the body is that, because of the limited capacity to store glucose, the body is programmed to convert the excess glucose into fat. This then creates its own side effects: obesity, for one. But more importantly, long-term hyperglycemia (diabetes) leads to numerous serious consequences: nerve damage to the eyes, legs, and/or feet—which can lead to blindness and limb amputations—and cardiovascular complications that lead to heart attack, stroke, and death.

When the role of insulin in juvenile-onset diabetes became clearer, it was referred to as "insulin-dependent diabetes mellitus" (IDDM) to differentiate it from adult-onset diabetes, which the diabetic experts renamed as "non-insulin-dependent diabetes mellitus" (NIDDM). Later, the medical community renamed childhood diabetes as Type 1 diabetes while adult-onset diabetes came to be known as Type 2 diabetes. Most people do not understand the differences between the two types, finding the naming conventions confusing. As you will learn in this chapter, Type 2 diabetes should not even be called by that name, as it is not a hormonal disease, but a lifestyle condition similar to diet-induced high cholesterol and would be better called "diet-induced high blood sugar." Type 1 diabetes should be called simply diabetes.

The Source of the Misinformation about Insulin Resistance

DeFronzo and his team's "insulin resistance" theory has become the universally accepted theory in the medical community to explain adult-onset diabetes. The problem is, the theory has not been proven to rigorous scientific standards. There is no data that shows why only three types of cells are supposedly "resistant" to insulin. No one knows how the resistance occurs or what causes cells to start becoming insulin resistant. There is no test to measure the degree of resistance at any one of these sites.

Dr. Falta's hypothesis that adult diabetes must differ from childhood diabetes was consistent with a scientific-minded researcher wanting to develop an explanation for the difference. It is good scientific thinking to wonder how elevated blood glucose and insulin could be present at the same time in a patient.

However, DeFronzo's claim was totally premature. It is a requirement for good science to ask for validation of a hypothesis using logic, verification of mechanism, and a reliable and reproducible test before it is accepted as fact. This is a common practice followed by all scientific disciplines.

There are many counter-facts that DeFronzo's conclusions about insulin resistance fail to account for or overlook completely. Let me present a few.

- DeFronzo claimed there was defective insulin secretion by the pancreas. His conclusion was based on the expectation that the pancreas should keep releasing the amount of insulin required to keep the level of blood glucose within a physiological range. What he failed to consider was that every bodily organ has an upper limit to what it can do, even under optimal conditions. Capping the maximum amount of insulin that the pancreas can produce might very well be nature's way of preserving the functional capacity of the organ or tissue that has to last a lifetime.
- DeFronzo failed to consider the possibility that the limit on pancreatic insulin secretion might also be an adaptive mechanism to prevent unhealthy consequences of too much insulin, such as weight gain or cancer cell multiplication, among others.
- His conclusion that muscles were not absorbing glucose failed to explain how supposedly starving muscle cells could continue to produce energy in a diabetic who is doing extreme or prolonged physical activity. Diabetic adults can still run, jump, play tennis, and dance. How could their muscles be starved with no glucose?
- He failed to provide any reasoning whatsoever for why muscle, fat, and liver cells would suddenly resort to ignoring the signals generated by insulin. These cells had no problems responding to insulin for decades in the earlier life of a person who developed adult-onset diabetes. Also, how was it that a diabetic's body had no problems responding to signals from other hormones, but just insulin?
- Most muscle activities occur in between meals when insulin level is at its natural low. Yet, the finding that blood glucose level becomes lower after exercise is used by endocrinologists as evidence of increased muscle responsiveness to insulin, induced by exercise. This explanation indirectly promotes the concept of insulin resistance as a causative factor for elevated

glucose level. What endocrinologists fail to clarify is that during exercise, muscles can activate another model of glucose transporter that does not require insulin's signal.

- Normally, insulin inhibits release of glucose from the liver. However, in Type 2 diabetes, the liver continues to release glucose even in the presence of insulin and this is presented as evidence of insulin resistance. However, DeFronzo's claim of impaired suppression of glucose output from the liver in the presence of insulin failed to consider the possibility that the liver could be responding to another signal outranking that of insulin: brain function. In human evolutionary terms, the liver may have been programmed to interpret continuous burning of fatty acids as a sign of deficiency of glucose as fuel for muscles and therefore compelled to keep producing glucose to provide fuel for vital centers in the brain which prefer glucose over fatty acids.

In short, DeFronzo appeared to have tailored the interpretation of his findings to justify the widely accepted concept of insulin resistance as the causative factor of Type 2 diabetes along with the gluco-centric approach by the medical profession when treating Type 2 diabetics. In this view, glucose control is thought of as being equivalent to diabetes control.

The Story of Insulin

Canadian researchers Dr. Frederick Banting and Charles Best were credited in 1921 with the discovery and administration of insulin to dogs (which had their pancreas removed to make them hyperglycemic). Before them, a few other researchers had also prepared pancreatic extracts that reversed the consequences of hyperglycemia, but Banting and Best also collaborated with researcher J.B. Collip, who purified the pancreatic extract and removed the potentially toxic substances that contaminated earlier versions of insulin. Equally important were the contributions of J.J.R. Macleod, who coordinated research and critically evaluated the design and results of experiments.

Another researcher, Elliot P. Joslin, while studying at Harvard Medical School, became interested in treating diabetes to help an elderly relative of his own who was diagnosed with it. He created a list of diabetic patients, complete with facts about their cases, their progress, and final outcomes. He published the first Diabetic Manual, to be used by doctors and patients, with an emphasis on educating the patient to take charge and feel empowered instead of victimized by the condition.

In 1923, two years after the discovery of insulin, Joslin recruited nurses to go out into the community and instruct people with diabetes about insulin, diet, and exercise. In 1927, after analyzing data from over 4500 diabetics, he reported that with the use of insulin, coma as a cause of death in diabetics fell from 61% to 20%. However, the incidence of arteriosclerosis had risen from 15% to 47%. He thus believed that persistent hyperglycemia is likely a cause for arteriosclerosis because the association was demonstrable in every adult diabetic who had glucose in the urine for 10 years or more. Joslin thought that "the chief cause of [the] premature development of arteriosclerosis in diabetes, save for advancing age, is due to an excess of fat, an excess of fat in the body, obesity, an excess of fat in the diet and an excess of fat in the blood." As he wrote, "Every dose of insulin you give your patient defers the advent of his arteriosclerosis, postpones old age."[10]

Dr. Joslin's dietary approach of reducing fat rather than carbohydrate, along with insulin injections, was not accepted by all medical practitioners. For example, Fredereick Madison Allen (1874-1964) advocated a carbohydrate-restricted, low-calorie diet for the management of diabetes. However, while Allen's patients got their blood glucose level under control through dietary modification without medications, they could not sustain his diet long-term.

After Joslin publicized how he reduced the death rate of his patients by tight control of blood glucose through diet, exercise, and insulin, his approach became the guiding principle of diabetes management. One reason is that patients found a low-fat diet easier to do compared to the low-carbohydrate diet of Allen's.

No one had sufficient data to challenge Joslin's views on diabetes management, or an alternate hypothesis to explain the development of hyperglycemia in adult-onset diabetes. The result was that gradually insulin resistance, defined as an impaired biological response to either exogenous (out-of-body) or endogenous (internal body) supplied insulin, emerged as the accepted cause of glucose intolerance leading to Type 2 diabetes.

Joslin's enthusiasm is totally understandable in light of his experience of saving hundreds of children from early death with injections of insulin and wanting to accomplish the same in adults with diabetes. In addition, he may have sincerely believed that the cause of high blood glucose must be the same regardless of the age of the patient. He could not have separated diabetes into two types because a test to measure blood insulin levels was not available at the time and he was therefore unaware of the fact that blood glucose was elevated in spite of the presence of insulin.

In the absence of a more scientifically valid study of the "insulin resistance" hypothesis, endocrinologists over the past decades have tried to show the validity of their glu-co-centric approach to treat diabetes using various clinical studies.

Misinformation After Type 1 Diabetes Study

The National Institute of Diabetes and Digestive and Kidney Diseases [NIDDK] funded the Diabetes Control and Complications Trial (DCCT), which took place between 1983 and 1993. Participants with Type 1 diabetes were treated with three or more shots of insulin per day or an insulin pump. They were asked to self-monitor their blood glucose level at least four times per day. The control group used only one or two shots of insulin per day with daily self-monitoring of urine or blood glucose. When the study ended after 10 years, an analysis of results showed that participants who kept their blood glucose level close to normal greatly lowered their chances of having eye, kidney, and nerve disease. This prospective study correlated clinical benefits of reduced diabetic complications with reduced blood glucose levels obtained through the administration of insulin in Type 1 diabetic patients, a validation of Joslin's concept.

However, the researchers were not able to show whether the group of people who used the more intensive treatment (3 to 4 shots per day or a pump) had lowered their risk of heart disease. This was perhaps because these participants were between the ages of 13 and 39, ages that are generally without hypertension or macrovascular disease. In addition, intensive therapy using insulin was associated with a three-fold increase in the risk of severe hypoglycemia (low blood sugar) and a 73% higher risk of becoming overweight (because insulin increases fat production from the liver).

Realizing the propaganda value of results obtained by Joselin's gluco-centric approach using insulin in Type 1 diabetics and its validation through DCCT, endocrinologists adopted the same approach to treat Type 2 diabetics. The immediate benefits were manifold. It established insulin use as a valid treatment to lower blood glucose level in diabetes before anybody could question its use in a person who purportedly is resistant to it.

Endocrinologists could now start any presentation on diabetes with a slide showing the confirmed value of insulin treatment in reducing blood glucose. Endocrinologists could also justify the creation of a cadre of certified educators along the line of nurses employed by Joslin, as I will explain shortly, to promote this approach to treat Type 2 diabetes. This allowed time to promote the myth of insulin resistance in Type 2 diabetes without validation of the concept through accepted scientific methodology and justified inclusion of Type 2 diabetes as an endocrine disease in medical textbooks. It created an argument to ask for money to do research in the name of getting clarity of the mechanism of insulin resistance in Type 2 diabetes and the role of a gluco-centric approach in diabetes treatment.

In fact, this effort was so convincing that the NIDDK created the Centers for Diabetes Translation Research in the name of accelerating positive impacts of research on population health with an emphasis on novel research. But, most importantly, it justified billing government health insurance programs and private insurance companies for treatments based on the gluco-centric concept of Type 2 diabetes.

Misinformation After Type 2 Diabetes Experiments

Although Joslin's approach of using insulin to treat Type 1 diabetes appears to have been validated, it became evident that, in the long-term, DCCT could not be used to fully justify the use of the gluco-centric approach using insulin to treat Type 2 diabetic patients.

Therefore, a few years later, a similar study was done using Type 2 diabetes patients. A total of 4,209 participants with recently diagnosed

Type 2 diabetes were randomly split up into two treatment groups: 1) a conventional treatment (diet only) and 2) an intensive treatment with oral medications (sulphonyl urea or metformin in overweight patients) or insulin.

At the end of the study, patients assigned to the intensive treatment experienced a risk reduction of 25% for any microvascular complications (related to arteriosclerosis). However, the benefit of reduced mortality and cardiovascular events was shown only for those who were overweight and treated with metformin. Just as in the Type 1 diabetes study, there was an increase in the incidence of severe hypoglycemia and body weight.

In another later study, called the Action to Control Cardiovascular Risk in Diabetes (ACCORD) using older and long-standing patients with Type 2 diabetes with high cardiovascular risk, the HbA1c test averaged 6.4% in the intensive control group vs. 7.5% in the conventional group. This suggested that the use of medications or insulin helps to reduce blood glucose levels. But even then, the primary outcomes (combined end-points of fatal and non-fatal myocardial infarction or stroke) were not significantly reduced in the intensive participants, despite having a 1.0% lower HbA1c than the other group. This study proved in fact that intensive glycemic control (using medications or insulin) can be harmful in many patients with longstanding Type 2 diabetes.

This finding should not have been surprising because hyperinsulinemia (too much insulin) is associated with an increased risk of hypoglycemia, hypertension, coronary artery disease, and stroke. This suggests that the benefits of being treated with the high doses of insulin that are frequently required to lower blood glucose levels to proper physiological levels could be associated with weight gain that exacerbates macrovascular complications. In fact, this is reminiscent of the threefold increase in arteriosclerosis described by Joslin in his study. In other words, too much insulin is actually a potential danger to Type 2 diabetics.

In summary, Joslin documented phenomenal success in improving the quality of life and prolonging the lifespan of certain diabetic patients, the vast majority of whom were children with Type 1 diabetes. He was able to correlate the degree of control of the disease with the level of blood glucose achieved through the administration of insulin. It was natural for him to promote this gluco-centric approach to anyone with diabetes. However, he had no knowledge or opportunity to differentiate Type 1 diabetes, a true endocrine disease, from Type 2 diabetes, which should be considered a lifestyle condition and not an endocrine disease due to the failure of the pancreas to produce insulin.

Yet, endocrinologists for decades now have been promoting the concept advanced by DeFronzo by repeatedly using the term "insulin resistance" when describing the genesis of Type 2 diabetes. This makes it appear to be more scientifically and medically legitimate and allows them to continue to classify it as a hormonal disease.

Endocrinologists give people the impression that the details of insulin resistance are only for them to understand; they fend off questioning patients with platitudes and seem either defensive or angry when you insist. Through repetition by several generations of endocrinologists and its incorporation into medical textbooks, it has come to be accepted as a "verified" concept and is relied on to justify using medications, including insulin injections, to control Type 2 diabetes. For example, the website of the National Institute of Diabetes and Digestive and Kidney Diseases (NIDDK) states, without providing any evidence or explanation: "Type 2 diabetes usually begins when muscle, liver, and fat cells do not use insulin well." There is truly no scientific proof of this.

Equally important is the fact that nearly all modern day endocrinologists, instead of admitting that applying the treatment advocated by Joslin in Type 2 diabetics was based on misinterpretation, are actively promoting the same misinformation to justify the gluco-centric approach to treat people diagnosed with Type 2 diabetes. While there is some degree of recognition that diet and exercise can help control adult-onset diabetes, the basic science behind it still reinforces the myth that it develops due to three types of cells becoming insulin resistant. Worse, this misinformation is resonated by many others who have significant vested interests in maintaining adult-onset diabetes as a disease, rather than a lifestyle condition largely caused by our modern diet high in grains.

The following sections identify the many groups and industries that have vested interests in keeping the nomenclature of Type 2 diabetes and the myth that it is caused by insulin resistance.

Certified Diabetes Educators

With the accepted characterization of adult-onset high blood sugar as "Type 2 diabetes" and the medical community labeling it a chronic "disease"—even leading people to think that it has a genetic component—there has come about an army of trained people who are licensed to help patients optimize "metabolic control," essentially meaning their blood sugar control. These people are called Certified Diabetes Educators. It is estimated that there are over 15,000 certified diabetes educators in the United States and another 15,000 diabetes educators in practice.

A Certified Diabetes Educator is a health professional who has received special training in diabetes treatment and education. To qualify as a Certified Diabetes Educator, or CDE, a health professional must have completed at least 2,000 hours of hands-on diabetes education and pass an examination given by the National Certification Board of Diabetes Educators. The exam covers a wide range of current knowledge in diabetes treatment and education. Generally, Certified Diabetes Educators are healthcare professionals such as nurses (RN), dietitians (RD), or pharmacists (RPh).

The medical community commonly assumes that the educational lessons provided by such diabetes care and education specialists can help people with Type 2 diabetes better manage their blood glucose, develop coping skills to address daily challenges of the disease, and reduce their risk of diabetes complications. These educators give advice on healthy eating habits through nutrition education, meal planning, weight-loss strategies, and other types of disease specific nutrition counseling. They offer courses on glucose monitoring, insulin delivery devices, insulin therapy, and various medications.

Unfortunately, for all their potential value, any evidence of benefits from their practice, such as avoiding the serious complications of diabetes—blindness, amputations, and premature death—is lacking. One reason is that they focus their definition of success purely on numbers, using improved glycemic indicators, such as the A1c test, as the yardstick for helping patients. In other words, with their emphasis on helping patients keep their blood sugar (glucose) levels in a healthy range, CDEs discuss how often to check blood glucose, how to do it properly, and how to interpret the numbers. This approach, in turn, solidifies the notion of blood sugar management as the main objective in the control of Type 2 diabetes.

The knowledge gap between science and CDEs comes down to an educational system where CDEs are instructed to follow guidelines to propagate the approved concept of diabetes rather than educate themselves on what insulin resistance is. Even those CDEs who want to learn are looking for information in a field they are not really trained to recognize science-based information versus misinformation based on biased interpretation.

In short, CDEs are expected to be the mouthpieces that amplify the message rather than, through critical thinking, question the veracity of what they are asked to do. This often results in intensifying the treatment of diabetes patients through medications and insulin injections, rather than through honest education about the role of diet and the importance of avoiding weight gain and obesity as the most important factors in controlling, if not reversing, diabetes. Yet more and more diabetes educators are recruited each year as the incidence of diabetes grows worldwide.

The Self-Monitoring Device Industry and Insurance Companies

According to the American Diabetes Association:

> Self-monitoring of blood glucose (SMBG) is an important component of modern therapy for diabetes mellitus. SMBG has been recommended for people with diabetes and their healthcare professionals in order to achieve a specific level of glycemic control and to prevent hypoglycemia. The goal of SMBG is to collect detailed information about blood glucose levels at many time points to enable maintenance of a more constant glucose level by more precise regimens. It can be used to aid in the adjustment of a therapeutic regimen in response to blood glucose values and to help individuals adjust their dietary intake, physical activity, and insulin doses to improve glycemic control on a day-to-day basis.[11]

Similarly, the Mayo Clinic generally recommends that Type 2 diabetics who use insulin test their blood glucose two or more times per day.

The sad reality is that this approach creates an illusion that just knowing blood glucose level at any given moment gives one control of Type 2 diabetes, while leaving any specific action needed to correct it to the discretion of the patient who may have no idea as to what exactly caused an unexpected elevation or an unanticipated lowering of blood glucose. In addition, many may become anxious for fear of immediate side effects related to a reading outside the normal range. There is no other chronic lifestyle condition where one is expected to monitor a nutrient level in the blood multiple times daily.

In addition, there are no studies based on sound scientific principles and clinical practices showing SMBG reduces the incidence of diabetic complications, improves quality of life, or prolongs the lifespan of Type 2 diabetic patients. In fact, studies have found that SMBG does not lead to better patient outcomes and has no effect on patient satisfaction or the patient's health-related quality of life. It appears that the chief beneficiaries of this practice are the manufacturers of these devices, practitioners who recommend them, and retailers who sell them, especially since the expenses are mostly covered by private health insurances, Medicare, and Medicaid.

My recommendation to those who have access to a blood glucose monitor is to use it to identify what type of meals contributes to your post-meal elevation of blood glucose. I call this Dr. John's food glucose test. Essentially, you would check your blood glucose prior to a meal and check it again around three hours after the start of the meal. Using the readings, you might be able to assess what component of the meal is most responsible and how you can lower the intake of that component to not only moderate post-meal elevation of blood glucose but also to control your fasting blood glucose, as I will explain later.

The Artificial Sweetener Industry

Another shocking example of misinformation in the management of Type 2 diabetes is the myth of substituting artificial sweeteners for sugar in daily life. Here's why this is a myth.

As I explained at the beginning of the chapter, glucose in the blood is commonly called blood sugar. It is understandable that the average person with no knowledge about the chemistry of sugar would be confused. The table sugar we use is actually sucrose, not glucose. People often think that by not using table sugar, they are decreasing their blood sugar. In fact, one of the first actions a person newly diagnosed with Type 2 diabetes tends to do is to stop using table sugar almost completely and to switch to using artificial sweeteners in their coffee, in soft drinks, and even in canned and baked goods. This is a complete misunderstanding about the meaning of "sugar."

Many of the foods that humans eat contain some kind of molecular form of sugar that eventually breaks down into glucose that enters the bloodstream to be used by cells for energy. But the sugars in our foods differ in their molecular composition, and that makes a difference in whether you overload your system with glucose or not. There are three forms of sugar that we commonly encounter:

- *Sucrose.* This form of sugar is found in fruit, berries, sugar cane, sugar beets, and other crops that can be boiled down into forms of sugar. Each sucrose molecule is composed of one glucose molecule + one fructose molecule. Fructose is absorbed only half as fast as glucose from the intestine and it must be converted into glucose by the liver before it adds to blood glucose level.
- *Lactose.* This form of milk sugar is found in dairy products. It is made of 1 molecule of galactose and 1 molecule of glucose. Galactose must be further processed by the liver before it can elevate your blood sugar.
- *Maltose.* This type of sugar is found in carbohydrates, including vegetables and grains. This form is composed of two glucose molecules. The most common example of an encounter with maltose is in ripe bananas, where the sweetness comes not from sucrose but from the breakdown of complex carbohydrate into maltose. The point to remember is that maltose is an integral part of complex carbohydrate molecules packed inside grain kernels. During a meal very little of the complex carbohydrate is digested in the mouth and therefore the presence of maltose is difficult to detect. This is why food items made from grains and grain-flour create very minimal sweet taste. This, in turn, creates the belief that by consuming grain one is not adding to the blood sugar. However, that glucose is released in the intestine where there are no taste buds located to inform the brain of the arrival of sugar.

What all of the above means is that grain-based food items like bread, pizza, or a slice of cake contain more glucose that will enter your bloodstream faster after digestion than if you ate a piece of fruit or a bowl of berries or even added some table sugar to your coffee.

The diabetes medical community does little to educate people about these facts about food choices and healthy diet relative to consumption of sugar versus grains. The truth is, there is hardly any evidence that an excess intake of added table sugar (sucrose) is directly linked to Type 2 diabetes, prediabetes, or cardiovascular disease. Furthermore, there is no evidence that strict avoidance of table sugar in quantities commonly consumed by the average person contributes to lowering blood glucose levels.

On the other hand, there is evidence to suggest that those who consume non-nutritive (i.e., having no nutritional value) sweeteners end up overcompensating in their eating habits due to the false sense of consuming less food energy from the sweetness they develop. Let me clarify. As mentioned above, nature combines sweetness with energy-containing food nutrients such as sugars. This means registration of sweetness by taste buds informs the control centers in the brain of the entry of nutrients in the mouth. In anticipation of the absorption of needed nutrients within a short period of time, the control center can reduce the intensity of hunger.

However, if the control center is informed of no absorption of glucose after the sensation of sweetness was received from the mouth, the sensation of sweetness coming from the mouth would be considered meaningless. This could lead to the control center waiting for other nutrient-associated signals, such as elevation of blood glucose which takes more time to reduce the intensity of hunger before terminating a meal. In short, rather than consuming natural sugar or food items like a piece of whole fruit, diabetics are led to believe that it is better for them to eat cookies, cake, pies, candies, and other grain-based desserts that were made with artificial sweeteners. In reality, these products may contribute to weight gain and obesity.

Yet, in general, endocrinologists, diabetes educators, and dieticians counselling Type 2 diabetic patients often overlook the patient's ignorance of the lack of connection between natural sugar and blood sugar. They promote instead, either directly or indirectly, the use of non-energy sweeteners. The position of the Academy of Nutrition and Dietetics even states that: "choosing NNS (nonnutritive sweeteners) instead of nutritive sweeteners is one method to assist with moderating carbohydrate intake."[12]

Of course, the biggest beneficiary of this myth appears to be the manufacturers and retail merchants of artificial sweeteners, who will continue to avoid truth-telling about the non-nutritive value of their products and the lack of proof that foods made with non-nutritive sweeteners are any better for the public than natural products like fruit.

Endocrinologists Who Endorse the Inheritance of Type 2 Diabetes

Many people diagnosed with Type 2 diabetes have at least one close family member with the disease. This has led medical practitioners to explain to their patients that they may have inherited diabetic gene(s). The seemingly logical explanation is that we all carry genes that allowed our ancestors to store energy to help them survive during long periods of starvation. When exposed to a sedentary lifestyle and the high caloric intake typical of the Western world diet, the same genes tend to make people obese.

Then, the theory goes, obesity combined with physical inactivity leads to insulin-resistant states. In addition, the hypothesis claims, the combination of insulin-resistance and the genetic burden place a major stress on the pancreatic beta cells to keep increasing their secretion of insulin to match rising glucose levels in the blood.

The problem with the genetic pass-down theory of diabetes is that it has yet to be proven. Despite all the research that has been done to decode the human genome, no one has yet to discover the gene or mutation that causes diabetes. The genetic theory of diabetes passed from one generation to another is misleading people to believe they have no choice in life—that if their mother, father, aunt, uncle, or grandparent had diabetes, they have a high probability of developing it. The family history of diabetes becomes a preordained destiny in their mind, as if they have no power to take care of their own health.

This view that diabetes is inherited is very likely false; in 50 years of gene research there has been no evidence to back it up. Although the advent of genome-wide association studies has led to the identification of multiple candidate genes, the genetic loci discovered to date explain only a small proportion of the observed heritability. In short, there is no clear pattern of inheritance of genes related to Type 2 diabetes.

Yet, the misinformation persists as endocrinologists continue to convince patients that they inherited their diabetes and they too will likely have the same destiny as their relatives. This perpetuates the gluco-centric treatment of diabetes that uses diabetes educators, pharmaceuticals, and insulin injections—still with no emphasis on changing the diets of patients.

The Pharmaceutical Industry

The best way to understand the current state of diabetes care is by taking note of the enormous contrast in scientific knowledge that has been developed in two areas. The first area is that of antibiotic/antimicrobial resistance, knowledge that has been gained over the past 80 or so years. Penicillin, the first commercialized antibiotic, was discovered in 1928 by Alexander Flemming. Eventually medical researchers noticed that germs like bacteria can develop an ability to resist the drugs that were designed to kill them. For example, penicillin-resistant Staphylococcus aureus was identified in 1942.

Bacteriologists then made great strides in identifying the nature of this resistance. As with any living organism, bacteria have a survival instinct and researchers identified that as the driving force behind the development of antimicrobial resistance. Bacteria develop their resistance mechanisms by using instructions provided by their genes. Furthermore, since the discovery of antibiotic resistant bacteria, many antibiotic escape mechanisms have been identified. For example, some bacteria are found to change or limit entryways into their cells, thereby restricting access of the antibiotic. Some germs create pumps to wash out antibiotic drugs that enter the cell. Some germs use enzymes that can neutralize antibiotics. Some bacteria modify or stop using the target sites that antibiotics attack to destroy them.

These types of research-based knowledge have enabled researchers to formulate new measures to overcome antimicrobial resistance. When it was found that the size of penicillin G is too large to enter certain bacteria, researchers were able to create ampicillin and amoxicillin, which are smaller and diffuse much faster. Furthermore, researchers have been able to change the basic structure of penicillin to make it evade enzymes secreted by bacteria. They have also created clear guidelines for using antibiotics, so as to prevent the development of antibiotic resistance by bacteria. Finally, researchers have been able to formulate ways to avoid the need for antibiotics by preventing bacterial infections in the first place.

Compare this to the second area of knowledge, which is that of so-called "insulin resistance." There has been a nearly total lack of knowledge developed in that area. Dr. Falta believed that a similar mechanism of resistance that bacteria use occurs in cells in the body, which could explain elevated blood sugar even in the presence of insulin in Type 2 diabetes. It was a logical supposition at that time.

However, endocrinologists have yet to learn much about insulin resistance in about the same space of 80 years. They cannot explain why certain cells, not all cells, in the body develop "insulin resistance." Researchers in diabetes have failed to even articulate, let alone establish, any explanation for why only three out of 200 different cell types in the body develop insulin resistance. They have no explanation for why among all hormones in the body, these cells chose insulin as their target to resist, and even then, only resist signals related to glucose entry. They tout the existence of insulin resistance in muscle, liver, and fat cells, but they cannot clarify a molecular mechanism of resistance in any one of these sites. Researchers have no test to measure the degree of insulin resistance at any one of these sites. They cannot show that glucose that is removed from the blood in response to insulin injected into the body or released into the body in response to a medication, actually allows blood glucose to enter cells that were supposedly resistant to insulin. Compared to bacteriologists, endocrinologists have made poor progress—the concept of resistance continues without reevaluation.

Instead, what the medical field of endocrinology has accomplished is to create different formulations of insulin, such as rapid acting (injected and inhaled), short-acting, intermediate acting, long-acting, and ultra-long-acting. In addition, they have created a new class of medications called insulin secretagogues that directly act on the patient's pancreas to cause secretion of insulin. This could be dangerous to the pancreas as it could cause it to overproduce insulin and to prematurely fail due to overuse.

Many other new diabetes medications for Type 2 patients are promoted based not on reduced incidence of diabetic complications compared to existing medications, but rather by claiming flexible dosing and less hypoglycemia compared to sulphonylurea while reducing HbA1c. In short, the drug industry is simply adding to its inventory of drugs to sell, not solving the diabetes problem at its core.

In short, 80 years after Dr. Falta's proposal, although there is a greater understanding of the science underlying the molecular pathways of insulin signaling, we are not anywhere near identifying the real cause or mechanism of this so-called "insulin resistance." Therefore, unable to formulate ways to prevent Type 2 diabetes, we are encouraged to continue the gluco-centric management of it based on a misinterpretation by Dr. Joslin.

Unfortunately, more misinformation about diabetes is being added every year or so. For example, it is now known that some people with Type 2 diabetes suffer multi-organ complications despite keeping their A1c near target levels using insulin. This is explained away as the result of a disease that is inherently progressive rather than a failure of treatment with insulin.

The most troublesome part of the gluco-centric approach using insulin is the false sense of empowerment the patient feels by being able to "control" blood sugar level by simply adjusting the dose of insulin. This disincentivizes the patient to the more arduous way of changing lifestyle to accomplish the same goal, even though this may negate the need for insulin. On the other hand, this approach incentivizes the pharmaceutical companies and gadget manufacturers to keep promoting the gluco-centric approach.

I believe that it is time to focus on the real cause and the right cure of Type 2 diabetes. The cause is the modern diet full of grains and grain-based products that overload the body with glucose and cause muscles to burn excess fatty acids rather than glucose, leaving glucose in the bloodstream. More of this view is explained in the box below.

A Primer on Energy & Fuels for the Body

How does the body create energy to power all your cells? The simple answer is food. If you don't eat food, your cells don't get energy and eventually die. So where does the energy that is stored in food come from?

The unit of energy used by plants, animals, and humans on earth is called Adenosine triphosphate, ATP. Plants harvest energy from the sun and create ATP, which is stored in molecules of glucose. Cells in our body can deconstruct glucose molecules thereby releasing the stored ATP to carry out metabolic activities.

Cells can't store a lot of glucose molecules because the amount of water needed to accomplish this would eventually stretch out cell walls and damage them. One way cells overcome this is by folding long chains of glucose molecules into a tighter form called glycogen which can be later dismantled to release the glucose as needed.

However, when there are excess glucose molecules absorbed after a meal, the body is programmed to store ATP in molecules of fatty acids that can store double the amount of ATP per gram compared to glucose. Fatty acids can be further compressed by creating molecules of triglyceride, commonly known as fat, that contain three molecules of fatty acids and one molecule of glycerol. Although the human body has no mechanism to reconvert stored fatty acid into glucose, it turns out that fatty acids can be dismantled to release ATP. Problem solved.

In other words, human cells can use either glucose or fatty acid to produce ATP needed for metabolic activities. In fact, the majority of energy produced during a day in the body, especially by muscles, comes from fatty acids rather than from glucose. However, certain cells in the body, such as nerve cells and mature red blood cells, prefer glucose rather than fatty acid as fuel for ATP production.

In addition, evolution endowed the liver to assist in glucose production. This was likely due to the fact that, periodically, humans faced famine with severe shortage of food intake. During these times, in order to protect the activities of nerve cells and red blood cells, the liver became endowed with the capability of creating new glucose molecules in a process known as gluconeogenesis. One of the raw materials used for this purpose is glycerol, released during the dismantling of triglyceride when muscles are burning fatty acid. The continued arrival of glycerol prompts the liver to keep producing new glucose molecules not only from glycerol but also from certain amino acids absorbed after a meal. This could explain how humans survived on whale blubber in the arctic regions for thousands of years without eating any glucose-containing foods for months at a time.

The importance of this is twofold. One, when there is an abundance of fatty acids in the blood, cells (especially muscle cells) could automatically switch to burning fatty acids, leaving glucose in the blood. I call this the "fatty acid burn switch." Secondly, the liver could keep fabricating new glucose molecules from glycerol and perhaps amino acids as well, adding to an already high blood glucose level, yielding to the evolutionary programming, and overriding insulin signaling to the contrary. I believe that this is the underlying physiological mechanism of continued liver production of glucose found in Type 2 diabetes.

In my opinion, the above observations can be used to support a new hypothesis to replace that of insulin resistance for the causation of adult-onset diabetes. In brief, the hypothesis is as follows. The body can easily release large amounts of fatty acids that had been stored as fat after the overconsumption of carbohydrates, especially grains. Muscles can then switch to burning these fatty acids for energy rather than glucose, leaving glucose in the bloodstream. This is the cause of high blood sugar (hyperglycemia), leading to Type 2 diabetes.

This explanation for Type 2 diabetes is far more biologically logical than the one based on the hypothesis of insulin resistance. It explains why any type of person can develop high blood sugar, even thin people. In fact, it also explains the genetic link to diabetes. What you inherit in your genes is your fat storage capacity, not a genetic mutation for diabetes (which has never been found). When your fat cells do not allow any further entry of glucose into them, it means they are at the fat storage capacity you inherited. This is why even a lean person can become diabetic, because he or she has less fat storage capacity, while an obese person may not become diabetic due to a larger fat storage capacity.

Meanwhile, the presence of insulin has no impact on liver cells to prevent them from releasing glucose. Rather, the liver continues to produce glucose, responding to its ancestral programming related to the perceived need to feed nerve cells (especially those in the brain) when it senses a high level of fatty acid metabolites in the blood, indicating that muscle cells have switched to burning fatty acids.

This theory also explains why pregnant women often develop gestational diabetes as they put on weight, fill up their fat stores, and begin burning the excess fatty acids. This also explains why pregnant women usually reverse their hyperglycemia within days of giving birth; they simply lose weight and empty their fat cells, reverting to a normal body metabolism of burning glucose.

How the Misinformation May Be Misleading You and How to Take Control

In the year 2020 there were over 122 million people diagnosed with elevated blood glucose in the U. S., 34 million with the diagnosis of Type 2 diabetes and 88 million diagnosed with prediabetes. You may have ancestors or living relatives with adult-onset diabetes and you may think that you too are destined to get it. Your doctor may tell you that you are pre-diabetic and that you need to begin taking medications. You may be putting on weight as you age and believe that it is just a little weight gain and there is nothing to worry about because there is no diabetes in your family history and none of your siblings have adult-onset diabetes.

All these conclusions are based on misinformation. You are being misled into believing in the insulin-resistance theory and the genetic inheritance theory of diabetes. The fact is, it is entirely in your hands to take charge of your life to prevent the development of adult-onset diabetes. Your diet plays the largest role in preventing high blood sugar. And your diet is something you can control.

In my opinion, this cavalier attitude of tacit acceptance has three serious consequences for tens of thousands of Americans who develop diabetes when it could have been controlled:

- Diabetes is unnecessarily damaging to the eyesight; it destroys the function of kidneys and damages the heart and brain.
- Diabetes results not only in the loss of productivity, but it also wastes the time and talent of caregivers, both in house and in institutions such as hospitals and dialysis centers, that could have been used for the benefit of others in need.
- Diabetes increases the cost of medical care for every American by virtue of insurance companies demanding more premium dollars in order to recoup the cost of care of those diagnosed with Type 2 diabetes and its complications.

Medicare Trust Fund Solvency

Medicare is the federal health insurance program for more than 60 million people ages 65 and over, and for younger people with long-term disabilities. It helps pay for hospital and physician visits, prescription drugs, and other acute and post-acute services. It accounts for 21% of national health-care spending and 12% of the federal budget. The Medicare

Hospital Insurance Trust fund from which Medicare Part A benefits are paid is projected to be depleted in 2026.

To address the shortfall between Part A spending and revenues, based on Congressional Budget Office's projections, a total of $517 billion in spending reductions or additional revenues, or some combination of both would be needed after 2026. I believe that we can go a long way to resolve this Medicare funding shortage by controlling Type 2 diabetes the right way. Let me clarify. The total estimated 2017 cost of diagnosed diabetes includes $237 billion in direct medical costs. If we could limit compensation for any Type 2 diabetes related medications, treatments, and gadgets to only those absolutely proven to reduce the incidence of diabetic complications or those needed to treat complications already diagnosed, we would achieve about 50% of the savings necessary.

People diagnosed with diabetes incur average medical expenditure of $16,750 per year, of which about $9,600 is attributed to diabetes. On average, people with diagnosed diabetes make medical expenditures approximately 2.3 times higher than what expenditures would be in the absence of diabetes. Today in America $1 out of every $7 heath care dollars is spent treating diabetes and its complications. For example, total Medicare Part D expenditures on insulin for diabetics increased 950% between 2007 and 2017, from $1.4 billion to $13.3 billion.

While insulin is a life saver for those diagnosed with Type 1 diabetes, it is a troublemaker for people diagnosed with Type 2 diabetes. Let me explain. The trouble starts with reduced quality of life related to the constant fear of low blood sugar and related complications including the possibility of dying. If a diabetic has experienced a serious hypoglycemic episode, any uneasy feeling, even an imagined one, could create anxiety about it happening again. This could lead to unnecessary food intake. Similarly, knowing that you might experience higher than expected blood glucose levels also creates anxiety. Some people may even try to be proactive and take extra insulin to prevent their blood glucose from rising.

This fear and anxiety among insulin takers create the perfect setting for exploitation by gadget manufacturers who promote the necessity of blood glucose monitoring. In addition, the family and friends of the diagnosed diabetic experience end up sharing in the anxiety, worrying about whether to invite the person for a meal, what to serve, when to start a meal and how they can be prepared to take care of a reaction related to their loved one's blood glucose level variations. For both the patient and family, travelling can also be a stressful event having to verify the availability of food on a timely basis and the need to be vigilant in case of a low blood sugar episode.

How to Overcome the Misinformation About Diabetes

Truth is the only proven remedy for misinformation. Therefore, to prevent the misleading information about Type 2 diabetes creating the above conditions, I suggest two solutions: one at the societal level and the other at the personal level.

At the societal level, I recommend the following:

- Endocrinologists and diabetic educators should be asked to show scientifically validated evidence to support their continued support for insulin resistance as the causative factor of Type 2 diabetes so that they are not suspected of promoting the concept to justify and preserve their income and/or livelihood.

- Educators of internal medicine and editors of medical textbooks should remove Type 2 diabetes from its current classification under endocrine diseases and recategorize it as an illness due to overnutrition in people whose fat storage capacity is filled, leaving glucose in the blood.
- The American Diabetic Association and the American Dietetic Association should explain how their actions and promotions help Type 2 diabetes patients rather than preserving their own self-interest.
- NIH and NIDDK should scrutinize all monies being allocated for research and treatment of Type 2 diabetes and its complications to make sure there is a solid verifiable scientific basis for those programs.
- Medicare and Medicaid should demand proof of benefit in terms of reduced incidence of diabetic complications before approving payment for services rendered to patients with Type 2 diabetes.
- Private health maintenance and health insurance companies should explain to their beneficiaries why they feel the need for continued collection of premiums and payment for continued care based on the prevailing hypothesis of insulin resistance.
- TV anchors and podcasters reporting on health-related topics need to question researchers and authors who are reporting on supposed "positive outcomes" in Type 2 diabetic patients used as study subjects. Their conclusions may be based on the acceptance of insulin resistance, without any evidence of that as the cause of Type 2 diabetes. This misleads the public.
- Writers and reviewers of articles should demand evidence of long-term benefits when they are writing about any new gadget or treatment for patients with Type 2 diabetes. A majority of Type 2 diabetes patients suffer some of the health consequences of diabetes despite their consistent treatments.

At the personal level, every person diagnosed with Type 2 diabetes has to realize that it is entirely in your hands to take charge of your life to prevent developing adult-onset diabetes. Your diet is the real cause and the right cure of Type 2 diabetes. The modern diet full of grains and grain-based products that overload the body with glucose and cause muscles to burn excess fatty acids rather than glucose, leaving glucose in the bloodstream is the cause of Type 2 diabetes. Simply lowering your intake of grain-based foods could lead to reversal of the condition.

The key dietary strategy is to get less than one-third of your total daily food energy intake from carbohydrates. Since it is not easy to be aware of the energy content of foods you eat, the simplest way to accomplish this is to stop consuming as much grain-based carbohydrate as the modern meal normally includes. Avoid eating grains and grain-flour based products at every meal. Cut down on breads, muffins, pies, cakes, doughnuts, pizza, tacos, and so on. Reduce your consumption of rice and corn.

Seek to cut your consumption of other foods containing complex carbohydrates (including potatoes) by about 50% of your current daily intake. Focus on eating fresh vegetables, meat, fish, dairy, and fruit. Such a variety will let your body absorb the needed nutrients in a timely fashion and moderate cravings that you may experience otherwise. Seek to keep your weight at its ideal level, about the weight you had when you were in your 20s, provided you had normal fasting blood sugar, cholesterol, and triglyceride levels at that time.

In short, an unproven hypothesis is the guiding principle of Type 2 diabetes management. Don't be misled by misinformation about adult-onset diabetes. It is a dangerous condition if you develop it and do not seek to reverse it through dietary change. Even if you follow your doctor's orders and begin taking medications and/or injecting insulin, you may still end up with the severe complications of diabetes—unless you take control of your diet.

Missing information in Type 2 Diabetes

As a final note in this chapter, consider the magnitude of effort needed to sustain the false concept of insulin resistance, given the absence of answers to a number of significant questions in the diagnosis and management of Type 2 diabetes. Let me cite some questions that demonstrate the lack of scientific logic in the insulin resistance theory. You are welcome to share this with your endocrinologist or diabetes educator if you have prediabetes or Type 2 diabetes.

1. Insulin is just one of about 50 different hormones that control a number of functions including metabolism, reproduction, growth, mood, and sexual health. What is the reason for the body to become resistant only to insulin and no other hormone?
2. Out of 200 different cell types in the body, only three are accused of non-responsiveness to insulin. Do different cells have an independent decision-making process when responding to insulin?
3. What is the mechanism that each cell type uses to not respond to insulin's signal?
4. The "insulin-clamp test," promoted as the gold standard proving the presence of insulin resistance, is based on interpretation of the data rather than actually measuring the degree of resistance. Why is there no test to obtain a direct measurement of the degree of insulin resistance?
5. Most adults at the time of diagnosis of Type 2 diabetes do not show any weakness of muscle performance. This indicates continued cellular energy production, in spite of their supposed resistance to insulin and reduced

entry of glucose. How do muscles continue to produce energy in needed quantities in spite of their inability to let glucose in?

6. Liver cells, supposedly resistant to insulin signaling, continue to manufacture fat molecules, a function carried out in response to insulin signaling. What explains this contradiction?
7. Fat cells, supposedly resistant to insulin signaling, continue to store fat, an action that requires entry of glucose under the direction of insulin into the fat cell so that it can manufacture glycerol needed to reconstitute a new fat molecule. What is the mechanism by which fat cells produce glycerol molecules?
8. It is unusual to prescribe the same medication to a person who is known to be resistant to it. What is therefore the rationale for why insulin is prescribed to a person who is supposedly insulin resistant?
9. In most instances of medical management of an illness, a medication found not to achieve the desired benefit is replaced with another one. In the case of Type 2 diabetes, oral drugs such as metformin or sulfonyl urea are continued along with the introduction of insulin or insulin secretagogues to control glucose levels. The explanation given is that this makes it possible to use less insulin to control insulin resistance. Where is the evidence to justify this common practice?
10. Even when a diabetic's blood glucose level, measured as A1c, is brought within acceptable levels using insulin-based treatments, many patients continue to suffer the complications of diabetes. Why?

11. According to one study, the incidence of diabetic complications in long-standing diabetes is as follows: 60% of patients suffer nerve damage known as neuropathy, 50% of patients suffer kidney damage known as nephropathy, 25% of patients suffer eye damage known as retinopathy, and 2.5% of patients suffer diabetic foot damage leading to amputations.[13] Instead of reevaluating the value of insulin resistance-based treatment, diabetologists intensify the same treatment. What is the rationale for this approach?

These are critical questions that endocrinologists are ignoring to answer each time they prescribe insulin and other Type 2 diabetes medications to a patient in a blind acceptance of the theory of insulin resistance without proper scientific evidence. For patients, these questions represent missing information.

Chapter 2 Takeaways

- Most people think that Type 2 diabetes is simply a state of elevated blood glucose; however, it is not a hormonal disease as we have been led to believe. In actuality, Type 2 diabetes is a dangerous lifestyle condition that can be controlled through diet if people are educated about it. The misinformation about Type 2 diabetes leads millions of people to neglect essential healthful diet advice and slide down a slippery slope into developing persistent high blood sugar and eventually diabetes, which they believe must be treated with drugs and insulin injections.
- Early researchers concluded that adult-onset diabetes develops when just three types of cells—muscle, liver, and fat cells—start "resisting" the presence of insulin. The insulin is there outside the cell, but the cell does not recognize its signal or respond to it, and thus does not allow the glucose to enter inside. This leaves glucose building up in the bloodstream—hence high blood sugar. The problem is, the theory has not been proven to rigorous scientific standards. There is no data that shows what causes cells to start becoming insulin resistant and why only three types of cells are supposedly "resistant" to insulin. No one knows the mechanism by which insulin resistance occurs in any one of the cell types purported to be resisting insulin. There is no test to measure the degree of resistance at any one of these sites.
- All modern day endocrinologists, instead of admitting that applying the treatment advocated by Joslin in Type 2 diabetics was based on misinterpretation, are actively promoting the same misinformation to justify the gluco-centric approach to treat people diagnosed with Type 2 diabetes. It is critically important to understand that control of glucose with

medications such as insulin does not mean control of Type 2 diabetes. In addition, many groups and industries have vested interests in keeping the myth that Type 2 diabetes is caused by insulin resistance, including certified diabetes educators, self-monitoring device manufacturers, insurance companies, artificial sweetener companies, and the pharmaceutical industry.

- Every person diagnosed with Type 2 diabetes has to realize that it is entirely in your hands to take charge of your life to prevent developing adult-onset diabetes. Your diet is the real cause and the right cure of Type 2 diabetes. The modern diet full of grains and grain-based products that overload the body with glucose and cause muscles to burn excess fatty acids rather than glucose, leaving glucose in the bloodstream is the cause of Type 2 diabetes. Simply lowering your intake of grain-based foods could lead to reversal of the condition.

CHAPTER 3

MISSING INFORMATION ABOUT BODY WEIGHT, DIETS, AND EATING FOR NUTRITION

ONE OF THE MOST glaring areas of missing information, in my opinion, is the role of body weight in affecting lifestyle conditions. For example, studies have shown that 85% of people with Type 2 diabetes are overweight. This suggests that being overweight is a major risk factor for developing Type 2 diabetes. However, only 30 percent of overweight people have diabetes.

The fact is that, although weight gain is associated with increasing amounts of certain types of fatty acids, glycerol, hormones, and other substances thought to be involved in the development of "insulin resistance," no clear reason has been given for cells in only three sites—the liver, muscle, and fat tissue—to be affected. In addition, no one has identified a mechanism that explains how cells in these sites develop resistance while cells in other sites escape the development of non-responsiveness to insulin.

Diabetes experts often point to the absence of clear understanding of the cause in other medical conditions as justification for promoting the insulin resistance hypothesis and the current gluco-centric management of Type 2 diabetes. While it is acceptable when writing a historical novel to incorporate the writer's opinion along with proven facts, treatment of a condition such as Type 2 diabetes should be based on solid evidence. There should be proof of better protection of limbs, organs, and life with the use of prescribed medications compared to simple lifestyle changes.

A Primer on Body Weight

Many components—bones, muscles, fat, organs, water, cells, and other tissues—contribute to body weight. During the first year of life, a child triples body weight. After that, during the toddler years, the rate of weight gain slows because of natural control mechanisms that match one's food intake more closely to the growing needs of the body. However, as they continue to grow, the eating pattern of most children is influenced by their family's eating behaviors, taste preferences, and their culture.

Starting in their teens, young people may expand their food preferences influenced by what they see on TV, in advertisements, and in movies. An important change that many may not notice is the change in the mechanics of eating, essentially how they eat. Time constraints due to the multitude of activities teens are involved in enforces limitations of time allocated for eating. In addition, the availability and affordability of foods often influence what the teen eats, such that food choices are not entirely based on what the body needs or when the body needs food. The quantity consumed is further influenced by eating foods that require very little chewing because they are mostly grain-based (such as muffins, pizza, sandwiches, doughnuts, etc.), and made more palatable with the addition of salt. The result is a gradual increase in body weight.

Until about their mid-thirties, a person may gain on average one or two pounds a year and later be able to lose a few pounds of weight without much effort. As one gets older, however, it becomes obvious that losing weight is harder and harder. At the same time, you begin to become aware of people around you having been diagnosed with Type 2 diabetes, cancer, and cardiovascular events. Your anxiety leads you to pay attention when your healthcare practitioner asks you to lose weight, and so you try. You find that it is not difficult to lose weight by changing your food habits either on your own or through an organized weight control program.

What surprises most people, however, is that any weight they thought they lost for good comes back within a short period of time after discontinuing the weight loss program. It is easy to assume that since they were able to lose weight once, there is nothing wrong with the program they were following. They conclude that they are at fault for regaining the weight. In the meantime, their healthcare practitioner informs them of elevated blood glucose, triglyceride, or cholesterol and asks them to start taking medications to prevent complications. Most people start the prescribed medications, albeit reluctantly. Over time, they begin to feel comfortable taking these medications because their healthcare practitioner gets comfortable with the level of glucose and cholesterol they are maintaining. They also realize that they can keep eating most of the foods they enjoy and use the medications to control their blood sugar.

The Missing Information about Diet, Authentic Weight, and Obesity

Let me inform you of the missing information in this scenario. First, in most adults after age 35, weight gain is the result of fat accumulation. Fat accumulation comes from the intake of excess food energy (calories) and therefore weight loss only happens if you reduce the intake of calories. This is why most weight loss programs work at first. But nearly all weight loss programs have an embedded flaw. They are not designed to ensure the intake of needed nutrients at the appropriate times, either in the short-term or in the long-term. This is why most people regain the weight either while still in the program or shortly after stopping it.

This is because the formula to maintain one's weight requires the intake of all needed nutrients in a timely fashion. If the weight-loss diet you are following has not provided enough nutrients for your body, when your body needs them, you are likely to experience cravings. This makes it difficult, if not impossible to sustain the diet. In other words, gaining weight back after losing it with a prescribed diet does not mean that you are at fault or unmotivated. It is, in my opinion, the fault of the program because the diet did not provide you with enough of the right nutrients for your body.

The next thing you need to know is that when you bring your blood glucose down using a medication such as insulin, that glucose does not leave your body. It may be out of the blood stream, which is why your blood sugar readings are lower, but most likely the glucose has been converted to fat by the liver. Similarly, when a medication lowers your blood cholesterol, it is most likely the result of inhibiting cholesterol production in the liver, but the raw materials are still in the body.

The best way to control lifestyle-associated conditions such as Type 2 diabetes, cancer, and cardiovascular events is to maintain what I call your "authentic weight," the weight that is appropriate for you based on your own metabolic activities, rather than on averages recommended by researchers. Your authentic weight is the weight at which blood glucose, triglyceride, and cholesterol are within normal range in the fasting state.

To understand this concept, let me clarify the evolutionary reason for forming and storing fat in the body. The body often has to consume more energy-containing nutrients because that may be the only way to get sufficient amounts of essential nutrients that are incorporated into the energy-containing nutrients. For efficiency of storage, excess energy consumed is converted into fat. Nature created fat tissue as a storage facility to prevent fat from adhering to arterial walls and causing blockages.

But can we store unlimited fat? The answer is no, because there is a biological limit to the number of cells any organ or tissue can produce during the life of an organism. Thus, the question is, how can you know what your fat storage capacity is and, more importantly, when you have filled it up? To answer this, you need to understand the following information.

The term "genotype" refers to the complete set of genes a person has. For practical purposes, all children in a family inherit the same set of genes from their parents. However, all siblings with the same genetic material don't have the same appearance or personality. Environmental factors and fetal growing conditions interact with the genes in question, starting in the womb, modifying physical and psychological traits.

For example, a fetus having an excess of nutrients in utero could influence the number of fat stem cells formed and the storage capacity of those fat cells, just as it might influence the bone size of the fetus. This means that each child can be born with a different fat storage capacity once all fat stem cells have been activated. This explains why one sibling might be thin and another heavier or bulkier in the same family, eating the same meals. This also explains why even when all members of a household consume excess energy-containing (high caloric) foods, one sibling may exhibit elevated blood glucose, a second child may have elevated blood cholesterol, while a third may have normal blood levels of both.

However, the other critical point to understand is that one's genetic capability need not translate into your destiny. By changing the molecular environment around genes through dietary manipulation, you can influence your health.

In my opinion, the best currently available clue regarding assessing the fullness of one's fat storage capacity is seen when a person has elevated levels of triglycerides, blood glucose, and cholesterol outside the normal range in the fasting state. Conversely, your body weight is "authentic" if those levels are within range, regardless of what standardized weight tables may say about your ideal weight. If you see your triglycerides, cholesterol, and blood sugar starting to rise, it means that you are moving outside of your authentic weight. You may be on a slippery slope to obesity, Type 2 diabetes, and/or cardiovascular disease if you let your weight, blood sugar, and cholesterol rise too high.

The Relationship Between Abdominal Obesity (A Pot Belly) and Type 2 Diabetes

Millions of years ago, to meet the body's need for energy, every cell could metabolize glucose, its primary fuel. However, during the further evolution of the cell, as the metabolic complexity increased, demand for energy also became greater. To meet this, cells needed constant access to fuel. In order to reduce the use of water to transport and keep glucose inside, cells found a way to use fatty acids that could provide double the amount of energy. The construction of the cell wall with fat molecules enabled cells to acquire fatty acids from the outside and burn them in the newly acquired internal power plant—the mitochondrion.

From the early days of infancy, fatty acids were stored as fat inside fat cells that could be kept in a central location, in the abdomen, from where fatty acids released could reach all parts of the body. Later, regional fat depots were created in the buttocks and breasts. In addition, a thin layer of fat cells under the skin served as insulation from the elements as well as a place to store additional fuel.

For any individual, the initial number of fat stem cells formed in the fetus depends on maternal nutrition. For example, in an infant born underweight because of maternal malnutrition, the number of fat stem cells is likely to be lower. Access to better nutrition during childhood can result in an increase in the number of fat stem cells. However, unlike stem cells that divide to create new cells needed for repair and maintenance of organs and surfaces, fat stem cells stop dividing after childhood. This creates a natural limit to fat storage capacity in adults. This is a key point in understanding the cause of Type 2 diabetes.

The fastest rate of growth experienced by a human being is in the first two years of life when the newborn baby more than triples in weight and grows longer. In order to obtain all the nutrients needed for this explosive growth, the baby consumes food, often taking in more food energy than can be used in between meals, because many micronutrients are embedded in energy-containing macronutrients such as complex carbohydrates, protein, and fat.

However, nature, well aware of this phenomenon, stores the excess energy in fat, resulting in the common appearance in infants of a pot belly, so that it can be utilized for subsequent growth. It is a common complaint of new mothers that the toddler is not eating much food compared to what the child was expected to eat based on her previous observation. Yet, the child appears to have no shortage of energy and, over time, as the child uses fat to produce energy, this pot belly disappears.

As you can see, abdominal obesity is really just a manifestation of energy consumed in excess. The problem is, as adults start to slow down in terms of energy use, the excess fat stored, regardless of its location, leads to other metabolic problems. Of course, the most obvious example of this is the pot belly and its association with Type 2 diabetes.

The evidence for this is clearly established. Many studies have correlated an association between abdominal obesity and Type 2 diabetes. However, the mechanism responsible for this connection between abdominal obesity and diabetes has yet to be clearly established. Some have suggested that local inflammation in adipose tissue leads to insulin resistance, though no specific reason for the presumed inflammation has been identified. Others have suggested hormones secreted by fat cells are responsible for insulin resistance, but again no mechanism by which these molecules influence cell response to insulin has been determined. Others point to the production of excess fatty acids induced by lipogenesis and fatty acid synthesis, as well as oxidated fatty acids. They claim that this is responsible for creating insulin resistance, but again, there has been no identification of the mechanism involved.

This is the use of one unproven hypothesis—the role of abdominal obesity producing insulin resistance—to support a previous unproven hypothesis—the role of insulin resistance as the cause of Type 2 diabetes. It is an excellent example of the use of one misinformation to strengthen another one about Type 2 diabetes. The proponents of these concepts absolve themselves by a simple sentence implying that the exact mechanism is yet to be determined, while expressing confidence in them.

In summary, endocrinologists, using medical terminology, scientific equations, and statistical analysis strive to promote a theory that they believe to be true but cannot prove. They try to convince Type 2 diabetes patients that there is no cure, so they must control their blood glucose level using a combination of lifestyle changes and medications. But the main beneficiaries of continued use of this paradigm as the basis to treat Type 2 diabetes appear to be pharmaceutical companies, which promote a variety of medications, as well as others who market blood glucose monitoring devices not only to the medical community but also directly to the public. Medical practitioners also feel pressured to oblige patients who believe that just by monitoring blood glucose level they are in control of their Type 2 diabetes, or, by reducing cholesterol and triglyceride levels by medications, they can prevent complications of Type 2 diabetes.

The net result of the insulin resistance theory is a serious reduction in the lifespan of people once they have been diagnosed with diabetes. Many suffer a significant deterioration in the quality of life, starting with the fear of hypoglycemia induced by diabetic medications along with varying degrees of diabetic complications suffered by different organs and systems in the body.

Don't get me wrong. I am not questioning the significance of abdominal fat accumulation related to the onset of Type 2 diabetes. That connection is true. My point is that the best way to prevent the development of Type 2 diabetes is to prevent continued accumulation of fat, regardless of the location of fat in the body, because you can develop Type 2 diabetes even without a pot belly. The talk about the lack of a cure for Type 2 diabetes by endocrinologists is, in my opinion, inexcusable without also telling the patient that the real reason for this assertion is their inability to find the real cause and the mechanism of "insulin resistance" despite more than 80 years of research. On the other hand, how can you cure something like insulin resistance that does not exist?

I suggest that you can prevent and reverse Type 2 diabetes by constantly monitoring two parameters. One is the daily measurement of your body weight and preventing it from going more than 5% above your authentic weight, especially after age 35. The second is by keeping your waist circumference in between one-half of your height and your hip circumference.

Learning to Eat for Nutrition, Not Fullness, to Avoid Obesity and Diabetes

In order to function optimally, the body requires over 100 different nutrients to be used by over 200 types of cells grouped into different organs and systems with specific functional arrangements. For example, bones need calcium while red blood cells need iron. Every cell needs an energy source and a waste disposal facility. Every organ needs mechanisms for receiving instructions in the form of chemical molecules called hormones or through nerves. All the systems and organs have to function in a coordinated manner and this requires a control center, in addition to control mechanisms that are regional.

Given all this, you may wonder: How can the body ensure intake of all needed nutrients in a timely fashion? Here is my analysis.

Missing Information about Why You Are Hungry or Full

As mentioned, the human body needs over 100 nutrients but there is no single food or food group that can provide all the necessary nutrients during one meal. This is the reason why we need to eat multiple meals composed of several items. However, even though the cells in the body are constantly using nutrients, the sensation of hunger is produced only periodically with unpredictable timing. How can this be explained? Let me illustrate with a few examples.

Baby animals of all sorts are capable of walking very early in life compared to human babies. They accompany their parents not only for companionship and protection but also to imitate and learn the art of food procurement. Newborn human babies, on the other hand, unable to move freely for the first few months of life, use two of their fully developed faculties, crying and sucking, to their advantage, without really understanding the sense of their actions. Once they realize the potential of these capabilities they use them to satisfy their needs, whether it is comfort, companionship, or nourishment. And, as they develop new faculties they follow the same adaptive mechanism of using existing capabilities to explore other possible benefits. This process of learning and adapting and then learning even more continues for the rest of life.

So learning starts from the moment you are born and continues throughout your life. Signals reach your brain from your eyes, ears, skin, receptors of taste and smell, and from organs and systems inside the body. These signals are analyzed, categorized, and stored in memory, not as a coherent single packet but in a long string of neurons, similar to a string of Christmas lights, located in different parts of the brain. They are accessible for recall of an experience when similar events activate the same member neurons, even if the current event is not directly related to the previous one. This type of storing and retrieval from memory is strengthened by repeated use but weakened by nonuse.

The brain functions in the same way when it comes to foods you learn to eat and enjoy. The subconscious mind of the brain keeps a real-time inventory of the nutrient availability in the body. At the same time, nutrient content of foods that have been consumed repeatedly to replenish needed nutrients are in the memory for reference. The subconscious mind can now create taste preferences for foods containing needed nutrients based on recognized deficits. This general pattern of inventory maintenance and source update is how the brain helps regulate our food intake; this regulation is based on current need and executed through the sense of hunger and satiation. Because of anticipation of multiple deliveries on a daily basis, this supply side management at the organism level minimizes the need for a large amount of shelf space to keep all needed nutrients in storage. Let me explain.

It is clear that we will consume water when we are thirsty. So how do you know you are thirsty? The answer is that the brain creates the sensation of thirst in response to signals received from various locations in the body regarding the lack of availability of water molecules.

In the same way, nutrient intake control centers in the brain receive information regarding any nutrients needed by the body's various organs and systems. When different organs and systems need different nutrients, the control center of the brain creates the sensation of hunger. It doesn't do this all the time, however, as then we would be eating all the time. The sensation of hunger occurs generally when the composite need for various nutrients reaches a certain threshold level. The body can withstand some nutrients being depleted for a while, but when the total need for a variety of nutrients goes high enough, the brain initiates the signal that food is needed. The variation in quantity and type of needed nutrients is why there is variability in the timing of our feelings of hunger.

Then, during a meal, a number of different nutrients are introduced into the mouth at the same time. How can the body identify these incoming nutrients? Even more importantly, how does the body make sure that a sufficient amount of the missing nutrients has been taken in? In addition, how can the intake mechanism be programmed to prevent excess intake of individual nutrients even when food is available in excess?

It appears that nature has perfected a nutrient procurement method called "chemical sensing" that is used by all living organisms on earth. For example, two plants growing side by side in the same soil absorb different nutrients in order to produce fruits or nuts of differing size, shape, texture, color, and flavor depending on their inherited genetic makeup. This is made possible by each root system identifying and allowing entry of needed nutrients dissolved in the fluid outside, identified through its chemical configuration.

In humans, one of the most important requirements for the chemical sensing system to work properly and ensure sufficient intake of needed nutrients is the association of nutrients with taste and smell receptors during a meal. Nutrients entering the body during a meal are detected and their quantity going down the throat are monitored by taste and smell receptors located in the mouth and nose (oral cavity). Embedded in these receptors are special types of voltage-gated ion channels that allow inward flow of sodium ions. These change the electrochemical gradient, ultimately resulting in the propagation of a signal to the nutrient control center in the brain.

An important requirement for the healthy functioning of the chemical sensing system is the signal travelling between sensors in the mouth and the control centers in the brain. Neurons in charge evaluate the incoming information and create a response. For example, when you consume a nutrient that is beneficial and in need at the time, the control center creates the sensation of enjoyment. Then when a sufficient quantity of that nutrient has passed through the mouth, the brain reduces the intensity of enjoyment. If you ever noticed that food doesn't taste the same on the 20th bite as on the 1st bite, this is why.

By the same token, when you consume something that is injurious, the brain can alert you by creating unpleasant feelings or even nausea. For this brain monitoring system to work efficiently, the signal traveling between the receptors in the mouth and the control centers in the brain has to function properly and fast. If you have ever put something that tastes foul in your mouth, you spit it out almost immediately, right?

If you stop to think about it, you will notice that nature packaged most foods from which adult humans can get nutrients from in forms that require chewing. This is because chewing releases nutrients at a speed that is favorable for registration by receptors in the oral cavity. To take full advantage of this system, one needs to eat slowly and chew each bite of food thoroughly. If the body has not yet consumed enough nutrients, the brain tells you to keep eating. If the incoming signals suggest you have consumed a sufficient amount of nutrients, the control centers in the brain create the sensation of satisfaction to terminate food intake.

Proof that We Eat for Nutrients

The presence of this human natural mechanism to ensure intake of all necessary nutrients has been amply demonstrated by a study done by

Dr. Clara Davis.[14] She allowed a group of toddlers to self-select different foods offered to them at meals. These toddlers were found to eat what they need in a timely fashion and in sufficient amounts to grow normally, even compensating for preexisting nutritional deficiencies.

For example, a toddler with a bone deformity called rickets, caused by poor calcification of the bone due to a dietary deficiency of vitamin D, voluntarily consumed cod liver oil, a rich source of vitamin D, until the bones healed. This amazing discovery demonstrates that the control centers in the brain knew what nutrient was deficient in the child's body, what food contained the needed nutrient, and how much was needed to rectify the condition. It was found that the child stopped drinking the cod liver oil when the bones showed healing as per radiographic examination.

Based on studies by Dr. Davis, in my opinion, there are three observations critical to understanding how the natural nutrient intake mechanism in humans works to help us eat the right amount and types of foods—if we allow it to guide us. We can see all three elements of our natural mechanism to eat in how toddlers eat once they are weaned and have teeth to chew foods.

1. Toddlers eat when they are hungry. Compare that to the present day food intake by adults. Most adults eat not because of hunger but because of other factors such as the aroma of the food, because it is time to eat according to their habit, wanting to please a host, food being served as part of a business meeting, at a celebration or party, or because of boredom or stress.
2. Toddlers choose to eat what they enjoy. In today's world, with limited time and resources available for procuring food, most people choose what to eat based on convenience of what's available and familiarity rather than for enjoyment of the food selected. This doesn't mean adults don't enjoy eating, but that they do not necessarily fully enjoy what they eat.
3. Toddlers stop eating when satisfied. Adults are more likely to continue to eat until the plate is empty for fear of wasting

> food. If food is free, such as at a party or company provided, or has already been paid for, such as at an "all you can eat" restaurant, most people are tempted to continue eating even after the enjoyment of eating has significantly subsided.

Compounding all the above poor eating habits that run counter to our natural eating inclinations that all toddlers exhibit is the easy availability of many foods that require practically no chewing. Eating foods that require little or no chewing leads to being able to eat them faster, effectively just swallowing them. These foods defeat the brain's signaling purpose of chewing and tend to facilitate the excess intake of food by reducing contact time with the receptors in the mouth. This method of eating, over time, may lead to eating to feel fullness of the stomach rather than a sense of satiation based on reduced enjoyment of food as the signal for meal termination.

Another impediment in regulating nutrient intake is the difficulty of the food intake control center to concentrate on the incoming signals from taste and smell receptors when signals reaching another control center have priority. I am referring to the brain center processing visual cues if you are watching an engaging television program while eating. The human brain, while aware of all incoming signals, can't concentrate on two significant events at the same time. So, if you combine eating with watching television, eating is conducted based on a preprogrammed pattern, which creates a strong possibility of overeating.

The Role of Cultivated Grains in Your Diet

After almost every presentation I give, I am asked by an audience member the following or a similar question: How can consumption of grain-based foods be harmful since for hundreds or even thousands of years our ancestors have been consuming various grains and grain-based breads, almost on a daily basis?

To answer that question, I suggest we need to think about the role of grains and grain-based foods at three levels:1) as a percentage of total dietary energy (caloric) intake per day; 2) the total energy intake in relation to your energy expenditure over a period of time; and 3) the expected age-related decrease in energy expenditure as one gets older. Let me explain.

Before the 1960s, it has been estimated that the amount of complex carbohydrate-based food energy consumed, mostly from tubers, grains, and grain-flour foods, was about one-third of total daily energy intake, on an average. Then, in the 1960s, the industrialized nations of the world experienced the "Green revolution," when grain farming and flour production were substantially improved due to new fertilizers and milling machines that made flour inexpensive. Following that revolution, the percentage of food energy consumed from complex carbohydrates was recalculated at about 50% in developed countries and about 70% in developing countries. These increases were due to various types of government help for farmers and distributors of grains and grain-products, and direct food-aid to individuals, families, and localities.

In the average family, the modern day diet is thus often grain-centered meals, containing foods requiring practically no chewing. Without chewing, it forces our sense of satiation to be determined not by a reduction in the intensity of taste in the mouth, but rather by fullness in the stomach as the primary determinant for terminating a meal. This has recently been further compounded by the popularity of blended and pureed foods in an attempt to consume more nutrients faster.

These factors have led, in my opinion, to the fact that more people are consuming more food energy each day than they can expend during a defined period of time. In developed countries, the availability and affordability of animal products may increase the total daily food energy intake, though it decreases the percentage contributed from cultivated grains. Nevertheless, the excess food energy consumed is stored as fat, and this is what leads to gradual weight gain and eventually obesity.

The problem is further compounded by age. As one gets older, there is usually a reduction in the expenditure of energy due to decreasing levels of hormonal support. Most seniors begin losing muscle mass, as well. Yet, most people, even in aging, continue to consume the same amount of food energy based on their long-term eating habits and cultural conditioning. This further leads to a gross mismatch between energy intake and energy expenditure over a period of time. The result is a further increase in body weight, paving the way for the development of lifestyle illnesses.

There is evidence to support this viewpoint. In an experiment with diabetic urban Australian aborigines, they were asked to move from their city to the bush and to revert to eating only what they could hunt and forage for, just as their ancestors did. During the study period, the participants moved from one food source to another, eating what was available in nature and not consuming any cultivated grains. At the end of the study, they were found to have lost weight and lowered their blood glucose and lipid (fat) levels.[15]

What I am suggesting is that as you get older, you need to better match your food energy intake to your decreasing expenditure of energy. The best way to do this is to limit your consumption of calories from grains and grain-based foods. This simple dietary change could help you avoid weight gain, obesity, and the potential to develop Type 2 diabetes.

The Role of Exercise in Lifestyle Conditions

Any book on prevention of lifestyle conditions would not be complete without a discussion on the value of exercise, because it is often promoted not only as a tool to prevent weight gain but also to lower blood sugar and avoid cardiovascular illnesses. Here are the facts, however, about what exercise can actually accomplish.

The value of exercise to prevent weight gain. On the surface, you would think this makes sense. When you exercise, your muscles send a message to the brain for additional fuel. The brain, in turn, sends a signal to the liver to release glucose not only to supply fuel to muscles, but also to brain cells. In addition, the brain sends another message to fat cells to release more fatty acids that can be burned as fuel, thus emptying them.

Given this biology, many people, especially those young in age, do lose weight using exercise as a tool. However, most people cannot rely on exercise as their primary method to lose weight. Here's why.

First, most people simply do not exercise enough. Exercising burns very few calories relative to one's daily intake, especially if you are already overeating. A woman weighing 140 pounds may expend 270 calories by walking 3.5 miles in one hour, 390 calories by riding a bike for one hour and going a distance of 10 to 12 miles, or 430 calories by running 30 minutes at a speed of 7.5 mph. But if she is doing one of these forms of exercise only two or three times per week, all the while consuming 1800 or 2000 calories per day, she will hardly make a dent in depleting her fat cells. The same goes for men, although the numbers are slightly different.

Another problem with exercise is that it does not have the same impact on weight loss as you get older. It is very difficult to keep up the level of activity needed to maintain a negative calorie intake when you have aging muscles. What used to take 20 minutes to burn 300 calories now takes 40 minutes or even an hour since there is a gradual decrease in the ability to maintain skeletal muscle function and mass.

Value of exercise to lower blood sugar. Most often, we exercise in the fasting state when the blood insulin level is at the lowest. However, active muscles can consume glucose without the help of insulin signaling and this leads to naturally lowering of blood glucose level. And, if you were able to achieve weight loss, you could prevent or reverse prediabetes and Type 2 diabetes. However, my opinion is that it is possible to lose weight through exercise and, in the process, reduce your blood sugar levels, but it is not probable for the reasons cited above.

Value of exercise in cardiovascular health. Exercise is valuable for one's health, because it not only conditions your heart and muscles but also your lungs. In addition, it prompts the heart to pump more blood with less effort than an unconditioned person. Conditioning allows your muscles to work longer before your brain senses the stress of exercise and makes you feel tired, compared to the brain that is not conditioned to exercising muscles. The ability of the human body to cope with unexpected events can be improved if the reserve capacities of vital organs are maintained.

Additional benefits of exercise come from improved blood circulation which helps the brain to think more creatively and the skin to have a better tone. The sustained elevation of body temperature you get from exercise also improves the immune system and defense mechanisms of the body and makes it easier for the transfer of glucose from the blood into active muscle cells, as you learned in the prior section. For many people, the addition of exercise in their daily routines also offers the key to greater psychological happiness and wellbeing.

In short, although regular physical activity reduces the risk of developing cardiovascular disease, Type 2 diabetes, dementia, and some cancers by at least 30%, physical activity does not promote weight loss. [16]

Therefore, for those who can maintain reduced weight through physical activity, they should pursue that until such time that it is not producing the desired health benefits.

Others may need a different approach, such as the one described in this book focused on a reduced intake of grain-based foods in one's diet. It is understandable that for many this could be hard because of significant variation from the traditional and familiar dishes made from grains that one grew up with. Sometimes, having support from family members or another group could be helpful. The best way to keep your motivation strong is to keep recalling the reward of not suffering from a lifestyle illness and its complications.

Learning Healthy Eating Habits

The information you have just read is generally missing from commonly given instructions on how to eat. This could explain why more than 42% of people in the U.S., as well as increasing numbers throughout the world, are obese. Another one-third of American adults are considered to be overweight. These conditions contribute to higher probabilities of lifestyle conditions.

Any time you think of food, remember that the body is looking for nutrients, not food groups such as carbohydrates, proteins, or fat. It is true that these food groups may carry needed nutrients but you have no clear idea what nutrients are lacking in the body when you feel the desire to eat. Every time you start eating, remind yourself to eat slowly and savor your food. Your brain's nutrient monitoring system detects not only what the body absorbed during a meal but also what was not acquired. If you can begin to apply this same thinking to all your meals, you will soon find yourself satisfied with a smaller volume of food at each meal. Be assured that you can consume more nutrients at a later meal.

You will also discover that most food items made with grains and grain-flour, such as rice, pasta, and bread, are by themselves not pleasing to eat. In fact, while upright humans have been on the earth for over 50,000 years, they only started eating cultivated grains in the last 12,000 years. This is nature's way of informing you that you can cut back on grains and grain-based foods without affecting your intake of nutrients needed for healthy living.

No matter what prompts you to start eating, if the default mechanism of meal termination is fullness of the stomach, it almost invariably leads to excess intake and the attendant lifestyle conditions of obesity, Type 2 diabetes, and cardiovascular disease.

Chapter 3 Takeaways

- Until about their mid-thirties, a person may gain on average one or two pounds a year and later be able to lose a few pounds of weight without much effort. As one gets older, however, it becomes obvious that losing weight gets harder and harder. What surprises most people who try a diet program is also that any weight they thought they lost for good comes back within a short period of time after discontinuing the weight loss program. The missing information here is that in most adults after age 35, weight gain is the result of fat accumulation that comes simply from the intake of excess food energy (calories). Weight loss can only happen if you reduce your intake of calories.
- When you bring your blood glucose down using a medication such as insulin, that glucose does not leave your body. It may be out of the blood stream, which is why your blood sugar readings are lower, but most likely the glucose has been converted to fat by the liver. The best way to prevent lifestyle-associated conditions such as Type 2 diabetes, cancer, and cardiovascular events is to maintain what I call your "authentic weight," the weight that is appropriate for you based on your own metabolic activities, rather than on

averages recommended by researchers. Your authentic weight is the weight at which your body has normal fasting levels off glucose, triglycerides, and cholesterol.

- In the average family, the modern day diet is often grain-centered meals, containing foods requiring practically no chewing. Without chewing, it forces our sense of satiation to be determined not by a reduction in the intensity of taste in the mouth, but rather by fullness in the stomach. This has recently been further compounded by the popularity of blended and pureed foods in an attempt to consume more nutrients faster. These factors have led, in my opinion, to the fact that more people are consuming more food energy each day than they can expend during a defined period of time. So relearn to eat as children do, eating only when you are hungry and pay attention to the reduction of taste in the mouth, not the fullness of the stomach. Being overweight invariably leads to the lifestyle conditions of obesity, Type 2 diabetes, and cardiovascular disease.

CHAPTER 4

MISSING INFORMATION ABOUT CANCER

Cancer is uncontrolled cell multiplication. The concept of uncontrolled cell division, which leads to uncontrolled cell multiplication in the body, becomes clear if you think about the process of controlled cell multiplication, which you already know because it occurs in everyday situations, such as when you cut yourself or fall and get a wound. The healing of a wound comes about through controlled cell multiplication.

So to understand cancer, let's start with some basic information on how cells multiply.

A Primer on Cell Multiplication and Genes

Stem cells are mother cells that are capable of producing new cells. The body is full of stem cells that were formed when you were an embryo. These cells were assigned to various organs in the body but sit in waiting throughout your life to be activated when they are needed to multiply to replace dead or dysfunctional cells.

When cells are destroyed, such as due to an injury, the surrounding cells send a message to the nucleus of the nearest stem cell. The nucleus contains genes that regulate each and every cell activity. The gene in charge of cell division issues a "work order" to create new cells. When a sufficient number of cells have been created to heal the wound, another gene issues an order to stop the cell division. This is how normal cell multiplication occurs: one order to activate cell division and another to stop it.

Each of us has two copies of every gene in the cell nucleus, one from each parent. If one gene is damaged due to a mutation or any other cause, the alternate gene takes over with that function, proceeding normally. However, if both copies of the gene in charge of a particular activity are incapacitated, that cell activity will stop. For example, if the gene pair was in charge of initiating the work order for healing a wound but had been inactivated, new cells may not be produced and healing may not happen. On the other hand, if both copies of the gene in charge of stopping cell division are damaged, the multiplication will go on and on in an uncontrolled manner, as long as construction materials are available. This is how cancer starts. As stated above, cancer is the uncontrolled multiplication of cells.

The Genetic Basis of Cancer

The average age of an adult with cancer is over sixty years. It is supposed that this is due to the amount of time it takes to accumulate enough gene mutations to create a cancer stem cell.

To understand the process of gene mutation, you need to know what genes are and how they regulate every cell activity. Within each cell, the nucleus contains 23 pairs of chromosomes. Each chromosome is made up of thousands of genes. Each gene is made up of DNA segments composed of nucleotides. These are an organic molecule consisting of a five-carbon sugar molecule, a nucleobase, and a phosphate group. Nucleotides are obtained in the diet and are also synthesized from common nutrients by the liver. The deoxyribonucleic (DNA) segments are constructed using two chains of nucleotides that coil around each other to form a double helix; this structure carries genetic instructions for the development, functioning, growth, and reproduction of all known organisms. These instructions are carried out within each cell through proteins that are manufactured within the cell following that cell's genetic code.

When cells multiply, the entire set of 23 pairs of chromosomes must duplicate so a new set of chromosomes can populate the new cell being created. However, errors can occur in that duplication process, such as an alteration in the nucleotide sequence. When an error occurs, it creates a mutation. When the new cell then divides, the existing mutation is then passed on to any new daughter cell. If an error occurs again, it creates a second mutation. In this way, cells can randomly contain many mutations that have arisen over time by chance.

The body is prepared to deal with cells with mutations. Tumor suppressor genes (TSGs) are in charge of hundreds of biological functions in each cell, including DNA damage repair, cell death, and cell division inhibition. I call TSGs "growth inhibiting genes" because they are in charge of stopping cell divisions that naturally occur, either to replace cells lost due to injury and infection or to replace cells lost to normal wear and tear.

It is thus clear how cancer could happen if the growth inhibiting genes are not working properly to stop the process of cell division. As this explanation points out, if you experience mutations of both copies of the growth inhibiting gene in a stem cell, you are prone to develop cancer when the stem cell starts dividing, because it cannot stop.

Not everyone may develop cancer from gene mutations. It takes a variable amount of time before mutations in both copies of the gene produce a cancer cell. Some people may have inherited gene mutations yet may not develop cancer until they accumulate enough to create a cancer stem cell and form cancer. Cancer-causing gene mutations can also develop from exposure to radiation, chemicals, infectious agents, and oxygen radicals. There are also random anomalies that occur when cells are dividing rapidly that can lead to gene mutations, resulting in the formation of a cancer stem cell, as during fetal development and during chronic inflammation and cell replacement. For example, it has been estimated that around 15-20% of all cancer cases are preceded by inflammation at the same tissue or organ site. The most prominent examples include inflammatory bowel disease (IBD), chronic hepatitis, and Helicobacter-induced gastritis increasing the risk of colorectal cancer, liver cancer, and stomach cancer, respectively.

The Fear Response

Receiving a diagnosis of cancer evokes at least two very strong emotions in the patient or in the parents of a child diagnosed with cancer: fear and helplessness. Fear is often due to thinking about the possibility that one might have continued exposure to the same agents that triggered the cancer in the first place. Fear also may be due to not knowing what the future holds in terms of one's lifespan as well as worry about how the diagnosis will affect family and loved ones. Keep in mind that the designation "cancer survivor" does not mean complete absence of cancer cells in the body but the absence of detectable cancer cells based on currently available testing methods.

Helplessness often stems from not knowing whether something you did or did not do was responsible for the cancer. People often feel helpless also because they are uncertain whether they have gotten enough detailed instructions about their treatment to prevent a recurrence, other than the common instructions to "eat a proper diet and get adequate exercise."

Three Critical Areas of Missing Information about Cancer

When it comes to cancer, there is actually an enormous body of information that is missing for most people in their understanding of what cancer is, how it causes death, and how you can survive it. Due to the vast amount of this missing information that people seldom learn, I cannot cover it all in this single chapter. I have therefore selected three key items of missing information that could help cancer patients or parents of a child with cancer to reduce the fear associated with being diagnosed with cancer. My focus in this chapter is to help readers understand what you are likely missing. These three items of important missing information are:

1. Cancer is well known to the body.
2. A cancer cell does not automatically become a cancer.
3. You have the power to control cancer growth.

Fuller knowledge of the above three issues could help reduce the consequences and complications of both cancer and its treatment. Let's look at each one.

Missing Information #1: Cancer is well known to the body

What does this mean? It means that the body knows that cancer cells form all the time and is prepared to deal with them. From the moment of conception, accidental mutations can happen, as explained above. But through evolution, the body has developed numerous mechanisms to deal with cancer cells.

If you think about it, there is a biological logic to this. The goal of all life is to survive. To survive, cells must divide because they do not live forever. The earliest cells that came into being on earth most likely were forced to divide due to internal factors, such as the increasing acidity that occurred in their normal functioning, because the cell had no reason or mechanism to divide based on external signaling.

The best example of how this type of cell multiplication happens is still evident in human life. Consider how a human being starts from a single cell, the zygote, which is formed after fertilization of the ovum. The zygote divides while travelling through the fallopian tube and, by implantation in the womb, contains over 200 cells. This could happen only if the zygote is responding to an internally generated signal since it is not yet connected to the mother during the travel time. In this process, I suggest that the zygote is expressing the cell multiplication process that had been inherited from the very first cells on earth, as explained in the last universal cellular ancestor (LUCA).[17]

Once the zygote is implanted in the womb, its cells continue to multiply at a very fast rate. By the time the fetus is formed, it contains 30 trillion cells. In that process, stem cells are assigned to an organ or bodily system and they then create the further cells needed for that organ or system. However, some stem cells are kept in reserve; they no longer multiply on their own. Instead, when they are assigned to an organ, they communicate through signaling, which tells them when to keep multiplying and when to stop. This continues to happen throughout our lifetimes each time some cells need to regenerate to produce replacement of cells lost after an injury or infection.

So what do I mean when I say that "cancer is well known to the body?" As explained above, the existence of mutations occurs all the time by accident as well as through a body's exposure to toxins and radiation that can cause mutations. The body is constantly fighting off these wayward cancer cells, and in general, it succeeds in preventing them from multiplying to the point of becoming a cancer tumor. This is why it usually takes decades for adults to finally develop cancer; the body is able to fight off cancer cells until enough mutations occur to overwhelm the body's anti-cancer mechanisms. (I will explain the body's mechanism to fight cancer below.)

You might ask, why do some children develop cancer? They have not lived long enough to have the degree of mutations that adults have when they get cancer. This can be explained through the following analogy. In the developing embryo, workers that construct new stem cells are all novices who can make mistakes during construction, such as in coding genes or by causing accidental dislocation of DNA sequences. It can also happen that cells in the fetus incurred a defect in the formation of the mitochondria within the cell, forcing the cell to revert to its ancestral way of dividing according to its own internal signals. Or a stem cell assigned to one organ may be displaced to an area where it could not respond to signals to stop the cell division. Sometimes the fetus or mother might be exposed to radiation or toxins that could also damage fetal stem cells. All of these occurrences could result in a newborn child having a cancer stem cell already "in waiting" at birth. In some children, unfortunately, that cancer stem cell in waiting develops into a full-fledged cancer.

Cell Division: An Evolutionary Perspective

The best way to understand uncontrolled cell division that is the hallmark of cancer is to study cell division from an evolutionary perspective. This knowledge could point to vulnerable sites that could be modified by new medical interventions, either to accelerate cell division to enhance healing or to slow down cell division to control cancer growth.

The survival instinct is the prime force driving the division of cells in all living entities. This is true for all forms of life, including acellular viruses, unicellular bacteria, and multicellular humans. What threat might have caused the earliest cell that appeared on this earth, which I call the Adam cell, to divide? Ordinarily, in an organism, cell division happens to fulfil a need, for example: to generate cells needed for wound healing; to regenerate an organ as in a liver transplant; to replace cells that have been destroyed due to wear and tear such as in the intestinal lining and skin; or to create cells needed to restore functional capacity after programmed removal of old cells, such as in red blood cells aged three months. None of these conditions were applicable in the case of the Adam cell. So what need did that first cell on earth have that forced it to divide? And whatever the need was, it had to be internal to the cell, otherwise the resulting daughter cells would have been exposed to the same external threat, with no net survival advantage by dividing.

I believe that cell division resulted from an increase in acidity within cells. This resulted from accelerated cell metabolism, which occurred when those early cells began metabolizing glucose to produce the energy needed for increasingly complex metabolic activities. Higher and higher internal acidity must have been the prime threat that forced some original cell to divide in an attempt to survive longer. Dividing into two cells lowered the acidity, allowing both cells to continue their existence.

Eventually, cells found a way to minimize their internal acidity by finding an alternate mechanism of producing energy. I am referring to the acquisition of mitochondrion inside the cell, a structure that acts as a power plant that can burn fatty acids to produce energy. This allowed cells to not only survive longer but also to stay together, rather than drift away from one another, as Adam cells were likely doing. The cells that were able to stay together became the Last Universal Cellular Ancestor (referred to as LUCA cells) that eventually evolved into higher and higher organisms until ending in human beings.

In summary, starting with the Adam cell, cells used their already existing capabilities to either develop or acquire new capabilities, all the while retaining many of their already existing beneficial capabilities. In fact, there are many examples of cells not only retaining useful capabilities but also activating them, some only temporarily, still evident in all living organisms. Here are a few of them to prove this point.

Producing energy from both glucose and fatty acids, which is practiced by every cell with a mitochondrion, is an example of this retained beneficial capability. Another one is that a zygote, the product of a sperm cell fertilizing an egg cell, exhibits cell division in response to only its own internal conditions while travelling through the fallopian tube. Once it is implanted in the womb, the cells in the embryo are programmed to divide as many times as needed to become part of an organ or system, and they no longer divide in response to their internal conditions. This transformation in the process of division is effectively proof of the capabilities cells once had to divide due to internal signals, probably high acidity as I theorize above.

Another evidence of the repetition of cellular ancestral programing is the retention of the capability to drift away from the site of production, as seen in the behavior of red blood cells and immune cells in the body. Equally indicative is the continued cohesion and collaborative working relationship of cells, as we see in organs. In both these cases, cell division happens in a programed fashion, controlled by the scope of need and supervised by genes in charge, both to start the process and to terminate it.

Now you can understand that when a cell starts to divide due to internal conditions, it is re-activating the ancestral response. This same process then has the capability to develop into a cancer if the daughter cells also exhibit the same propensity to divide. In another scenario, if both copies, one inherited from the father and the other from the mother, of the gene in change of terminating cell division become incapacitated, it could also result in uncontrolled cell division and the formation of cancer if the daughter cells also have the same damage. The first one is likely to be the cause of a majority of childhood cancers and the second that of adult cancers because a child has not lived long enough to accumulate mutations that incapacitate growth inhibiting genes.

The objectives of learning this evolutionary nature of cancer formation in the body are:

1. To understand the fact that, unless you have been exposed to known cancer-causing agents such as radiation or had chronic inflammation, the trigger that led to the formation of a particular type of cancer is most likely unknown. This also means that your cancer is not due to what you did or did not do.
2. The human body is well aware of the emergence of cancer cells from time to time simply from mutations and other biological accidents that take place during normal cell multiplication. Moreover, the immune system is very capable of dealing with it. But cancer happens when there is an accelerated multiplication of cells compared to the capability of the immune system to destroy them.
3. Understanding the cancer process allows you to use the vulnerability of cancer cells to your advantage by denying them the needed materials, energy, and support for multiplication. This part is augmented by limiting the number of cancer cells in the body through the use of approved cancer treatments that reduce the number of cancer cells.

4. Under the influence of confusion and uncertainty, common when dealing with cancer, a person often has to decide on treatments that may not have been fully evaluated. Knowledge of the cancer process allows the patient to make a more informed decision.

Missing Information #2: A cancer cell does not always become cancer

It is easy to understand that there is an abundance of precancerous cells in a fetus and, as we discussed above, adults may carry many cells with mutations that could become cancer. But this next piece of information is surprising to most people: a cancer cell does not always become cancer. This is why the majority of children do not develop cancer.

The body has several powerful anticancer mechanisms. They include the following three processes: gene editing, apoptosis, and the natural killer cells that are part of our immune system. Let's look at these.

1. *Gene editing and repair.* Ancient cyanobacteria often sustained damage to their DNA from environmental stresses, during starvation, or from internally generated reactive oxygen radicals. Nature therefore endowed them with numerous mechanisms to repair this damage using internally available replacement parts or through the uptake and incorporation of DNA from their surroundings (called exogenous DNA). The acquisition of exogenous DNA not only restored the structural integrity of the cyanobacterial DNA but it often incorporated new capabilities that had been encoded in the newly

acquired DNA. This process, in turn, could have contributed to the evolutionary advantage we now carry, that our cells can often repair damaged genes by re-editing an incorrect DNA sequence.

2. *Apoptosis.* This term refers to the self-destruction of a wayward cell. The body may fight off cancer cells by calling for them to self-destruct if the gene editing and repair did not work. Apoptosis is the process by which a member cell of an organ or system is destroyed for the sake of saving the whole so that nonfunctional cells do not clog up the passageways or interfere with the function of organs. It is estimated that, on average, 50 to 70 billion cells are removed each day due to apoptosis in an adult. In children between the ages of 8 and 14, the number is approximately 20-30 billion cells that die per day. During the process of apoptosis, the gene in charge activates the production of enzymes that degrade the proteins that form the structural and functional components of a non-functional cell. The component proteins can then be reused in other gene repair, or further degraded into amino acids that become part of the nutrient pool in the body. This is recycling at the molecular level. However, as you can imagine, excessive destruction of cells in an organ could degrade the functional efficiency of the organ. Similarly, an ineffective apoptosis could lead to uncontrolled cell proliferation and cancer.
3. *Natural Killer Cells.* Humans can escape external threats using intuition, reasoning, and visual and auditory cues. It is different when the threat is internal, such as an infection or cancer. During an infection, cells in the immune system can distinguish, detect, and identify an offending agent from among the cells that rightly belong to our own healthy tissues. This identification may be based on recognizing the whole infective agent as foreign, or on detecting specific protein parts that have already been identified from prior encounters with the

same or similar pathogen. In addition, the immune system could also be alerted by toxins released by the agent or by contents released from the damaged cells.

For simplicity, the immune response is generally classified into two actions: 1) *humoral*, as in producing antibodies, and 2) *cellular*, as in sending in white blood cells to battle the invading agent. In the first effort, when the immune system detects an infective agent, it sends out antibodies, which are proteins that seek to identify the cells that do not belong, such as bacteria, viruses, parasites, or fungi. The antibodies attach themselves to those cells to mark them to be destroyed. Some antibodies can attach to immune-system compounds that can kill the infective agent.

The second action of the immune system is the use of white blood cells to attack the invading cells. Within the group of white blood cells called lymphocytes, there is a subgroup called Killer T-cells that kill the targeted cells that are infected or dysfunctional.

The problem is, when it comes to cancer, these natural killer cells are at a disadvantage because the cancer cells appear to be normal members of an organ or body system. They look and function like normal cells, consuming nutrients and fuel just as any cell does. In the early stages of cancer formation, cancer cells do not show any structural defects that could be identified by natural killer cells nor do they release any telltale proteins. Cancer cells are not known to release toxins or destroy the neighboring cells by attacking them.

Even when cancer cells have formed a small tumor and, through their constant uncontrolled multiplication, they begin pushing away cells in the immediate vicinity, the immune system can be fooled enough to think that it is simply an expanding organ. Only when an obstruction in a natural passageway caused by an expanding tumor, or by increasing pressure inside a closed space such as the skull, or by decreasing space available for other cells as inside bone marrow happens, might the body be alerted to the presence of cancer.

This characteristic allows tumors such as ovarian and breast cancers to grow without being identified for a long time. In my view, it also suggests that society should put more effort into learning how to prevent cancer than in treating it, since treatment of many cancers cannot begin until they are noticeable, by which time it may be too late. The best way to accomplish this, in my opinion, is not to allow cancer growth to overwhelm the existing capabilities of the immune system.

Mechanisms I have described above and others in the body are powerful enough to prevent cancer in most children and adults. Understanding how they work will help you realize why the third piece of missing information is so important for anyone who has been diagnosed with cancer.

Missing Information #3: You have the power to control cancer growth

Have you ever wondered how cancer causes death since it does not release toxins or attack other cells in the body? The answer is that cancer deprives the cells of vital organs in the body of the nutrients they need for their functioning. This starvation at the cellular level can in turn lead to the functional derangement of key organs in the body. That is what leads to death.

The key to controlling cancer is therefore to try to prevent cancer cells from multiplying faster than the body's defenses, especially the immune system, can destroy them. I suggest it is literally possible to limit the rate of cancer cell multiplication through specific actions that you are in control of.

But, first, let me explain the concept of stem cell in waiting. Starting from birth, the body is full of stem cells that wait for the appropriate signals before starting to produce baby cells. Stem cells get activated at random; some frequently, some after waiting a decade or longer, and some never. The most common example is the body's production of replacement cells by stem cells in the intestinal lining and the skin to replace cells worn out by wear and tear.

We also see it in stem cells creating new red blood cells to replace those that are being taken out of service every three months, as well as replacements for white cells destroyed during an encounter with infective agents.

However, some stem cells may wait for decades and others may never get activated during one's lifetime. For example, stem cells in charge of producing breast buds are present at birth. Only at puberty do they start producing cells needed to form a breast, in response to hormones released from the pituitary and the ovary. In males, the absence of these hormones prevents the development of breast tissue, except in rare instances (called gynecomastia) when a hormonal imbalance stimulates the growth of breast tissue in males.

The missing piece of information here is the awareness that the progression of a cancer stem cell to cancer need not be automatic and inevitable, as you may believe. That progression is amenable to intervention and control. Thus, there are three important pieces of information that you should know about: the roles of 1) glucose and 2) insulin in assisting cancer growth, and 3) how you can improve your immune system through your choice of foods.

Glucose: Why You Need to Limit Carbohydrates If You Have Cancer

Cancer cells thrive on glucose. They voraciously absorb it. However, cancer cells are actually quite inefficient in utilizing glucose as fuel compared to how normal cells extract energy from glucose. This inefficiency appears to be an inheritance from the original cells that inhabited the earth when all cells lacked the power generation facility called mitochondrion that is seen in modern day cells. As you can imagine, cancer cells without their mitochondria have to revert back to their ancestral way of power generation, hence the appearance of inefficiency. But enough power is produced to proceed with cell multiplication. In addition, cancer cells can use the remaining parts of the glucose molecule to build new cells.

There is no doubt that cancer growth is positively associated with the availability of glucose. A person who consumes a lot of carbohydrates that digest into voluminous amounts of glucose is effectively feeding their cancer cells. A person with excess glucose constantly in the bloodstream, such as a diabetic, is also at great risk of feeding cancer cells in the body. (This is why there is a significant correlation between people with diabetes and the occurrence of certain types of cancer.)

The present day diet with an abundance of grain-based carbohydrates provides the glucose that cancer cells crave. If your diet includes a large consumption of carbohydrates, and you are concerned about developing cancer, or already have cancer, I suggest that the current evidence is a strong signal that a lifestyle change is necessary. Decreases in your plasma glucose levels may reduce your overall cancer risk. Hence my recommendation is that you limit your intake of carbohydrates to provide less than 35 percent of your total daily energy intake.

The Role of Insulin in Cancer Growth

As discussed in the prior chapter on misinformation about diabetes, insulin is a hormone produced in the pancreas that is utilized to alert cells that glucose is available outside. The role of insulin is to promote the uptake and utilization of glucose. Insulin can't make value judgments as to who is using glucose and for what purpose. For example, during a bacterial infection, the evolutionary benefit goes to the bacteria when there is excess glucose in the environment and insulin may even aid the uptake.

In a viral infection, it is the infected cells that are absorbing glucose and insulin is designed to promote cellular activity that involves glucose utilization. The result is, even though diabetics are no more prone to catch a virus such as Covid-19, once inside a cell, the virus can multiply faster and cause a more severe disease in a person with Type 2 diabetes than one without. In addition, insulin has long been known to also stimulate cell division. Many cancer cells create insulin receptors on their exterior surface whose activation in responding to insulin can be classified into three categories: survival, proliferation, and cell growth.

Therefore it is conceivable that high levels of insulin released by the pancreas in response to elevated blood glucose from the diet or from medications administered directly to control diabetes could promote cancer growth. Animal studies show a clear functional role for insulin receptors in breast cancer progression and metastasis.

Improving Your Immune System

We cannot leave the topic of cancer prevention without suggesting ways to improve the immune system that, given a chance, could keep cancer cells from destroying your health. One of the first instructions that will be given to you by you specialist after the diagnosis of cancer is to eat a balanced diet and get plenty of exercise to keep your immune system strong. You may even get instructions as to how many servings of carbohydrate, protein, vegetables, and fruits to eat. What you won't get is a list of specific nutrients to consume that could help you to strengthen your immune system, because the specialist has no way of knowing how your immune system became weakened or what nutrients you truly need.

Meanwhile, you may soon start getting advice from friends, family members, and well-wishers about various foods and nutritional supplements they recommend with "proven" capabilities to enhance the immune system. You might also see advertisements for many products in social media. However, unless you have been diagnosed with a specific nutrient deficiency, none of these could be of much benefit to you. They are nearly all misinformation or disinformation.

The best way to keep a robust immune system is to provide your body with all necessary nutrients in a timely fashion. Of course though, when you sit down to eat, you have no knowledge of what nutrients are lacking in the body. Yet, toddlers seem to be able to consume the necessary nutrients in a timely fashion, as long as a variety of foods are available to them. Therefore, my recommendation, which I call the rule of three, is for you to make sure that you consume a minimum of three different vegetables, three different fruits, and three different nuts every day. Vegetables, fruits, and nuts are the best sources of the micro-nutrients that the body may need.

My goal in this chapter has been to bring attention to the fact that many people are missing vital information about cancer. There is much more for you to learn, which is outside the scope of this book. But I am sincere in suggesting that, especially if you have a family history of cancer, there are many steps you can take to prevent cancer from occurring. If you have already been diagnosed, you have a better chance of survival if you take control. It begins with reducing the availability of glucose and insulin to cancer cells, by reducing your consumption of grain and grain-based foods found in the present day diet, foods that yield the maximum number of glucose molecules. In my view, that is one of the most important principles in surviving cancer.

Chapter 4 Takeaways

- Cancer is uncontrolled cell multiplication. When cells multiply, the entire set of 23 pairs of chromosomes must duplicate so a new set of chromosomes can populate the new cell being created. However, errors can occur in that duplication process, creating a mutation. When the new cell then divides, the existing mutation is then passed on to any new daughter cell. If an error occurs again, it creates a second mutation. In this way, cells can randomly contain many mutations that have arisen over time, quite by chance. If a mutation occurs in the growth-inhibiting gene, cells will keep dividing. That is cancer.

- Not everyone may develop cancer from gene mutations. It takes a variable amount of time before mutations in both copies of the gene produce a cancer cell. Some people may have inherited gene mutations yet may not develop cancer until they accumulate enough to create a cancer stem cell and form cancer. Cancer-causing gene mutations can also develop from exposure to radiation, chemicals, infectious agents, and oxygen radicals. There are also random anomalies that occur when cells are dividing rapidly that can lead to gene mutations, resulting in the formation of a cancer stem cell, as during fetal development and during chronic inflammation and cell replacement.
- Through evolution, the body has developed numerous mechanisms to deal with cancer cells. The existence of mutations occurs all the time by accident as well as through a body's exposure to toxins and radiation that can cause mutations. The body is constantly fighting off these wayward cancer cells, and in general, it succeeds in preventing them from multiplying to the point of becoming a cancer tumor. This is why it usually takes decades for adults to finally develop cancer; the body is able to fight off cancer cells until enough mutations occur to overwhelm the body's anti-cancer mechanisms
- My goal in this chapter has been to bring attention to the fact that many people are missing vital information about cancer. The key to controlling cancer is to try to prevent cancer cells from multiplying faster than the body's defenses, especially the immune system, can destroy them. I suggest it is literally possible to limit the rate of cancer cell multiplication through

specific actions that you are in control of—particularly your diet and keeping your immune system strong. Reducing grain consumption if you have cancer is vital to avoid feeding cancer cells with glucose and insulin, a cell growth promoter. Eat a wide variety of foods to ensure your immune system has all the nutrients the body needs.

CHAPTER 5

THE ROLE OF MIXED DMMI IN CARDIOVASCULAR DISEASE

TRUE SCIENCE IS NOT pretending what we practice is perfect. The hallmark of true science is constantly challenging what is accepted and then changing what is practiced based on new evidence that is discovered through research. The search for truth forces scientists to acknowledge their own limitations while endeavoring to constantly challenge health-related practices that they find to be not quite right.

One of these practices that should be of interest to a majority of people is how medicine has come to understand, explain, and treat cardiovascular disease. In this chapter, I will use the impact of our diets high in cholesterol, whole grains, and sodium to explain how both misinformation and missing information have misled millions of people to misunderstand the care of their cardiovascular conditions.

A Primer about the Heart

The term cardiovascular refers to the heart, a four-chambered pump made of muscle and blood vessels that is the plumbing of the body that carries blood out to every organ. Each of its components can be affected by a person's lifestyle conditions individually, consecutively (one after another), or concurrently (at the same time).

Following is a summary of how the cardiovascular system works: The left ventricle sends blood carrying nutrients and oxygen to every cell in the body. The aorta is the main vessel that carries blood from the heart. Branches of the aorta called arteries supply blood to every part of the body. Arteries divide further into smaller blood vessels called capillaries. Along the capillary walls are perforations or tiny holes that allow the fluid part of blood carrying nutrients but not the red blood cells to leak into the outside and reach nearby cells. (However, red cells get out when there is injury to the capillary wall, causing bleeding. White cells can also move out when openings are created in the capillary wall by enzymes released during inflammation.)

The fluid coming from the blood allows each cell to pick up needed nutrients based on the requirements of their functional specialization. Cells, in turn, discharge waste and carbon dioxide into blood that is returning to the right side of the heart.

Chances are you have never thought about blood returning to the heart from different parts of the body, even against gravity, for example, from the legs, compared to the heart sending it there by the force of the heartbeat. This return is aided by contractions of muscles that act as pumps to push the blood through blood vessels called veins. To prevent the blood from dropping back under the pull of gravity, veins have valves spaced at different intervals. It is when these valves fail that you see the bulging, as in varicose veins. This also means that if you remain immobile for extended periods of time, as during air travel or if you are bedridden, blood can stay stagnant, leading to the formation of blood clots that could be dangerous.

Veins empty the blood into the right ventricle. The right ventricle pumps blood to the lungs where carbon dioxide is released into the air and oxygen is picked up. The oxygenated blood returns to the left side of the heart to repeat the cycle.

As you can see, the cardiovascular system has to really work very well for every cell to perform its intended function at peak efficiency.

A Primer on Cholesterol

It would help if we also understood a little more about the role of cholesterol in the body. Cholesterol is a fat molecule that the body uses to synthesize steroid hormones, bile acid, and vitamin D. It is also an essential structural component of all cell membranes in animals. Plants do not produce cholesterol. A human male weighing 150 lb. normally has about 35 grams of cholesterol, mostly contained in the cell membranes. The typical daily dietary intake of cholesterol for an adult male in the U.S. is 307mg.

As a component of the cell wall, cholesterol serves as an insulating material, to prevent loss of heat when the ambient temperature is cold and loss of water when the ambient temperature is warm, in relation to the temperature of the body. This means that even those who eat only vegetable-based foods need cholesterol for healthy living. So, since plants do not produce cholesterol, how do vegetarians acquire cholesterol?

In every human being, the liver has the capability to manufacture cholesterol using a molecule known as acetyl coenzyme-A that can be derived from fat and fatty acids in the food or produced from glucose absorbed from carbohydrates in the food.

In 1977, the senior senator from South Dakota, Sen. George McGovern, chaired the Senate committee that investigated the increasing incidence of heart attacks experienced by Americans and issued a directive considered to be the precursor of the more detailed "Dietary Guidelines for Americans," a federal review of nutrition and health that is published every five years. Sen. McGovern relied on Dr. Mark Hegsted, a Harvard nutritionist, who had been studying fats and their role in promoting heart disease. In the early 1960s, Dr. Hegsted had experimented with dietary changes and their effects on levels of harmful cholesterol in the bloodstream. He and others investigated the role of saturated fats derived from meat, eggs, and other sources, as well as polyunsaturated fats and monounsaturated fats on dietary cholesterol.

Dr. Hegsted correctly identified cholesterol as the main culprit in causing blockage of the artery and, relying on his research experience, recommended that Americans eat less fat, less cholesterol, less refined and processed sugars, and more complex carbohydrates and fiber. His team also developed a mathematical model, known as the Hegsted equation, to predict the effect of fats consumed in food on an individual's serum cholesterol. This model started a fundamental shift in the diet of Americans and later in other countries, launching the popularity of low-fat diets with emphasis on whole grains.

Misinformation Regarding Good and Bad Cholesterol

It is now generally accepted that elevated levels of cholesterol play a role in the genesis of cardiovascular events such as heart attack and stroke. For example, cholesterol molecules can adhere to the interior wall of an artery if the surface is uneven after cells lining the wall sustain injury or experience inflammation. More cholesterol molecules could then be added, eventually causing a blockage of blood flow. When this happens in the artery that supplies blood to the heart muscle it is called a heart attack; when it happens in the artery that supplies blood to the brain, it is called a stroke.

Although the role of cholesterol in causing blockage of arteries is clear, misinformation about the real role of "good" and "bad" cholesterol is almost universal. You are probably familiar with those two terms, but not sure what they really mean in terms of your health.

When you have a cholesterol test, the doctor usually gives you the results referring to three parts: 1) total cholesterol; 2) HDL or high density cholesterol; and 3) LDL or low density cholesterol. HDL cholesterol is promoted as "good" cholesterol. Many people believe that the goodness of HDL comes from its ability to remove LDL cholesterol sticking to the arterial wall, and thereby preventing further cholesterol deposition that might eventually lead to a blockage in a blood vessel that impedes blood flow.

The misinformation here is the explanation of how "good" cholesterol removes "bad" cholesterol from its attachment site. HDL flows through an artery at an average speed of 3 to 4 mph. How can it know where the deposition of LDL is, change the direction of its movement towards the LDL, attach itself to the LDL and, most importantly, pull it off the arterial wall? Imagine that you stick a piece of self-adhering tape representing LDL on the surface of a table, with the table representing the arterial wall surface. Imagine sticking another piece of tape representing HDL onto the first tape. How can the second tape generate the energy needed to pull the first one off the table? Similarly, an HDL molecule does not have power to remove the LDL from the arterial wall. Only cells, not molecules such as HDL, can produce energy. In short, this hypothesis about HDL is misinformation.

In fact, some studies have shown that very high levels of "good" cholesterol may be associated with an increased risk of heart attack and death.[18]

Missing information about Cholesterol

When Dr. Hegsted suggested reducing fat intake to lower the cholesterol level in the body, he did not seriously consider the possibility that the liver could keep producing acetyl coenzyme-A from the very glucose absorbed from the complex carbohydrates that he was recommending people to consume more of. This glucose could later be converted to cholesterol by the liver. This meant his recommendations to eat more carbohydrates were incorrect.

This piece of missing information—about cholesterol made from glucose absorbed from complex carbohydrates—leads millions of people today to rely on medications prescribed by medical practitioners to control high levels of cholesterol or triglyceride in the blood, as high levels of cholesterol still result, in spite of a person reducing fat intake. Medical practitioners feel justified prescribing increasing levels of medication because they rationalize that their patients are not able to adhere to dietary restrictions, and, bottom line, the practitioners have an obligation to do everything in their power to prevent cardiovascular complications due to elevated cholesterol levels.

At the same time, patients continue with their usual diet, feeling comfortable that all they have to do to control their high blood cholesterol level is to continue taking cholesterol-lowering medications. In short, what is missing is a clear understanding of the factors underlying the elevation of blood cholesterol.

This mix of misinformation and missing information about cholesterol, as discussed above, is today driving an enormous profit-making industry that seeks to maintain the myths about HDL cholesterol. Prodded by their medical providers, pharmaceutical companies, food supplement manufacturers, and others, most people remain unaware that good HDL cholesterol offers limited protective effects.

The medical industry fails to provide a clear understanding of the role of HDL cholesterol and has been leading people to associate it with being a "good" type of cholesterol to have, without any real proof of this assertion. Based on this misunderstanding, scores of books, websites, and social media postings promote supplements, diets, and other remedies purported to elevate the level of "good" cholesterol in the body, believing that what they are doing is going to help.

A Primer on Grains

Most people hear the term "whole grain" but do not really know what it means and how it differs from any other type of grain listed in the ingredients of prepared foods. When grain is grown and harvested for foods, a kernel of whole grain contains all its layers: the endosperm, germ, and bran. This is in contrast to grain that has been refined and contains only the endosperm, which is then ground into flour. The difference in what gets milled determines if the resulting flour was made from whole grain or refined grain, as the two flours differ in their nutrient value. While the bran of a grain kernel contains 43 grams of fiber per 100 grams of grain, the endosperm contains only 4 grams. The more fiber in the flour, the longer it takes to digest, which helps slow the release of glucose into the body. Whole grain also contains more B vitamins compared to refined flour made only from the endosperm.

In the U.S., two to three servings of whole grain per day (one serving equals 30 grams) is considered the minimum recommended intake to obtain reductions in one's risk of negative lifestyle conditions. According to the American Heart Association in 2016, dietary fiber from whole grains, as part of an overall healthy diet, may help improve blood cholesterol levels, and lower the risk of heart disease, stroke, obesity, and Type 2 diabetes.

The Misinformation about Whole Grains

Misinformation regarding the consumption of whole grain comes from incorrect information about the role of the fiber ingredient that imparts the perceived benefits of whole grains. With no clear identification of the specific beneficial ingredient contained in the whole grain, or the mechanism of benefit delivery, consumers are led to believe that in order to obtain the desired benefits, they have to consume whole grains in prescribed quantities. But few people realize they can obtain the same nutrient from other sources, such as nuts and seeds. You do not need to eat food items made with whole grain to obtain beneficial ingredients associated with fiber.

According to the European Food Safety Authority (EFSA), the health claims about fiber— regarding weight control, management of blood glucose/insulin levels, healthy bowel function, blood cholesterol, satiety, glycemic index digestive function, and cardiovascular health—are not accurate. They say that "the food constituent, whole grain (. . . .) is not sufficiently characterized in relation to the claimed health effects" and that "a cause and effect relationship cannot be established between the consumption of whole grain and the claimed effects considered in this opinion."[19]

Missing Information about Whole Grain Consumption

There is also missing information in the promotion of whole grains. Consumers are seldom aware of the enormous amount of glucose they are consuming. Did you know that 100 grams of whole grain contains 77 grams of glucose from which the liver can produce either triglyceride or cholesterol (based on one's genetic makeup)? In effect, eating a sandwich, a slice of pizza, a doughnut or muffin, and so on—even if it is made with whole grain—floods your body with glucose that, if not used immediately by your muscles and organs, ends up getting stored as fat or raising your cholesterol level.

This mix of misinformation and missing information, as described above, misleads people into believing that they should eat whole grain foods. Added to this problem are the incentives from federal and local governments, community food assistance programs, and intensive marketing from for-profit private companies that make it possible for most prepackaged and convenience foods available for average consumers to be made with grains (whole or refined).

The result of this is that the average person in the U.S. (and in many other Western countries) is now consuming 50-70% of their daily food energy intake from grain-based items, compared to less than 35% of daily energy 100 years ago when people ate far more vegetables and fruit. In my opinion, it is the excess consumption of endosperm, whether from whole grain or refined grain, that is at the root of the increase in many lifestyle conditions—including obesity, Type 2 diabetes, and cardiovascular disease.

The Paradox of Agricultural Subsidies

The U.S. Federal government gives incentives to agribusinesses and farmers to supplement their income, manage the supply of agricultural commodities, and influence the cost of commodities such as wheat, maize (corn), barley, oats, and rice, among others. The Agricultural Adjustment Act (AAA) of 1938 was the United States federal law designed to boost agricultural prices by reducing surpluses. Today, the government pays around $25 billion every year to farmers in direct subsidies as "farm income stabilization."

While this subsidy supports the livelihood of farmers, in my opinion, as the program is currently designed, this is what makes it possible for cheap foods to be made from abundant grains and grain-flours, which ultimately contributes to the consumption of complex carbohydrates and the increasing incidence of Type 2 diabetes.

Redirecting the farm subsidy away from grains and more towards vegetables, fruits, and nuts could potentially reduce the incidence of Type 2 diabetes. This, to me, is logical, because subsidizing healthier foods will make their prices more competitive with grains. In the long-run, this redirection of subsidies would lead to a reduced incidence of Type 2 diabetes and could also reduce the stress on medical insurance programs such as Medicaid and Medicare.

In addition, if people were to begin eating more fresh vegetables and fruits, it would contribute extensively to reducing the newly diagnosed medical condition known as "obesity with malnutrition" that is showing up in some developing countries where multinational companies are promoting sales of cheap grain-based foods. When families in these nations can afford only cheap grain-based foods, the results are unquestionable as we see large populations who are overweight and/or obese while also being malnourished.

A Primer on Sodium

The body needs less than 500 milligrams of sodium per day to function properly. This is the amount in less than ¼ teaspoon! The American Heart Association recommends no more than 1,500 mg per day for most adults. However, on average, Americans eat more than 3,400 milligrams of sodium each day, with more than 70 percent of sodium consumed coming from packaged, prepared, and restaurant foods—not from the saltshaker. The problem is, after repeated intake of high levels of salt, you develop cravings for salty foods. You can easily get into this type of craving by eating packaged solid foods because they contain salt to increase their palatability and to prolong shelf life.

Misinformation about Sodium (Salt) Intake

The Recommended Dietary Allowance (RDA) is the estimated amount of a nutrient per day that is considered necessary for the maintenance of good health by the Food and Nutrition Board of the National Research Council/National Academy of Sciences. The RDA is updated periodically to reflect new knowledge.

Today's food labels nicely show us the amount of sodium in the product. The total sodium content on the label is supposed to include all forms of sodium; that should include sodium from salt plus that from any other sodium-containing ingredient, such as sodium citrate, monosodium glutamate (MSG), or sodium benzoate.

But here's where misinformation comes in. In general, the amount of sodium shown on food labels is not based on the amount of salt per day considered necessary for the maintenance of good health but as the percentage of the maximum amount an adult could eat on average daily. For example, 125 milligrams per serving may be listed as 5% of the daily value. Most people are unaware of this and may conclude that since the percentage shown is small, there is no harm related to salt intake in consuming the item of food.

Labels may also say something like "serving size 4 pieces" with sodium content of about 200 mg, as part of a long list of ingredients. The consumer, without really understanding the significance of this, or having no time or patience, may think that the label has been approved by some responsible government agency and therefore it is alright to consume the product.

The tragedy is most people do not understand these labels and shop strictly based on convenience. Canned goods, deli meats, and frozen products often contain voluminous amounts of sodium, far past the daily requirement. For example, some spicy pickles may contain 710 mgm of sodium per one tablespoon serving size. The worst part of this practice is that the information on the labels is not specific to children; giving young children prepackaged, convenience foods can hook them on high salt foods for the rest of their lives.

On October 13, 2021, the U.S. Food and Drug Administration (FDA) released new guidelines aimed at reducing the amount of salt that Americans consume at restaurants, school cafeterias, and food trucks, or when eating packaged and prepared foods at home. The aim is to reduce sodium intake by 12 percent over the next three years. This is intended to be the first step in a multi-year campaign to gradually lower the nation's sodium intake so it more closely aligns with the current Dietary Guidelines for Americans, which suggest a healthy diet should contain no more than 2,300 milligrams of sodium a day. Lowering sodium intake by about 40 percent from the current level could save 500,000 lives, the FDA said. Susan Mayne, director of the FDA's Center for Food Safety and Applied Nutrition, said more than 95 percent of children 2 to 13 consume more sodium than is recommended.

Missing Information about Salt

The fact that people fail to learn enough about high sodium intake could contribute to two unwanted consequences: high blood pressure and the impairment of one's natural nutrient intake regulation. A brief review of blood pressure is presented in the following box and that of the regulation of nutrient intake is presented after.

A Primer on Blood Pressure

As mentioned earlier, blood vessels are like a closed plumbing system that carries liquids. The presence of moving fluid inside the tube, similar to water inside a hose, imparts pressure on the walls of the blood vessel. Each time the heart beats, more blood is added to the circulation and the pressure increases based on the volume of blood ejected from the heart.

You may have noticed two numbers when your blood pressure is written down, the upper called *systolic* and the lower number called *diastolic*. The systolic number refers to the pressure reached after systole, or heartbeat, and the diastolic refers to the pressure in between. For example, if your blood pressure is 120 over 80 (120/80), it means that after the heart pumps once, the pressure reaches 120, then relaxes to 80. Normal blood pressure should be below 120/80. People are considered to have Stage 2 high blood pressure (hypertension) when their reading is 140-180/90-120.

Missing Information about Sodium and Blood Pressure Elevation

One of the main reasons for blood pressure elevation is an increase in blood volume. Most people do not understand how this happens.

When there is an elevation of sodium content in the blood, the body starts to retain more water to keep the sodium concentration within physiological limits. This is due to the body's need to maintain a certain sodium level for other physiological functions such as signal transmission, which I will discuss further shortly. The immediate effect of increased blood volume is elevated blood pressure.

This is because, when the heart beats, in order to pump blood out, it has to generate pressure higher than the prevailing pressure in the circulation. The higher the blood pressure, the higher the strain on the heart. Ultimately this could lead to heart failure. Control of blood volume through reduced sodium intake is one thing everyone can do to avoid unnecessary medical management of high blood pressure.

People may recognize that they have been gradually increasing their salt consumption. What they often fail to see is that they are making a lifelong habit of consuming high salt content foods. Their lack of success in efforts to cut down and control their salt intake points to an addictive behavior pattern that seems impossible to reverse. It is not, however. Anyone can learn to reduce their salt intake. What is missing is the information from animal studies that show that by gradual reduction of salt intake, the body can learn to restore its sodium balance, and thereby reduce the necessity or level of blood pressure medications.

Missing Information about Sodium and the Regulation of Nutrient Intake

We eat to obtain nutrients needed to produce energy and for growth and well-being of the body and mind. The physiological mechanisms that control your nutrient intake are established even before you are born. You start acquiring nutrients from your mother's womb. As a newborn baby, you survive solely on breast milk or formula and later add small amounts of pureed food. As the digestive system improves, finger foods are introduced, usually around 8 months. The diet is still limited due to the lack of teeth necessary to chew and grind, until about 18 months when both the teeth and the digestive system are sufficiently mature to handle the same foods as adults.

Then as adults, people fall into the routine of having usually two to three large-size meals per day, with variable intervals in between. Often snacks of smaller amounts are consumed in between meals. It is estimated that the average requirement for an average adult is between

1800-2000 calories (kcal) per day. A well-balanced meal which consists of the correct proportions to provide needed nutrients is considered to be one on which the plate is one-half vegetables, one-quarter protein-containing food such as meat, and one-quarter carbohydrate.

Keep in mind that when you sit down to eat you have no way to know what specific nutrients your body needs at the time. Yet your subconscious mind can direct you to pick food items, especially vegetables, fruits, and nuts that, based on previous experience, could provide the needed nutrients. The quantity needed is to be determined as you eat.

In short, to ensure the intake of needed nutrients in a timely fashion, without overeating, the oral receptors in the mouth have to function as they were programmed to. In this regard, sodium plays a key role in the nutrient regulatory system, because, as mentioned earlier, sodium is intimately involved in signal travel through nerves in the body.

The importance of this signaling process can be seen when you eat certain types of cucumbers. Some cucumbers produce chemicals known as cucurbitacins that make them bitter. However, salt reduces our ability to taste bitterness, not by neutralizing the bitter-tasting chemical but by making it difficult for the human brain to perceive the bitter taste. In effect, by interfering with the signaling mechanism, salt can interfere with the regulatory mechanism of nutrient intake.

What is yet to be clarified is whether interference of signal travel by an elevated sodium concentration in the body extends to communication between neurons in the brain. This could potentially not only contribute to impaired regulation of food intake but also to other cognitive functions that require concentration and response.

Chapter 5 Takeaways

- The average consumer is not only fed misinformation but is also sometimes missing vital information about cholesterol, whole grains, and sodium intake as they relate to cardiovascular disease as well as other lifestyle conditions such as obesity, Type 2 diabetes, and perhaps impairment of cognitive functions as you get older.
- It is now generally accepted that elevated levels of cholesterol play a role in the genesis of cardiovascular events such as heart attack and stroke. Although the role of cholesterol in causing blockage of arteries is clear, misinformation about the real role of "good" and "bad" cholesterol is almost universal. The misinformation here is that "good" cholesterol (HDL) removes "bad" cholesterol (LDL) from its attachment site; this hypothesis about HDL is misinformation. This misinformation has led millions of people trying to boost their HDL through supplements or other actions but not change their diet.
- At the same time, patients continue with their usual diet, feeling comfortable that all they have to do to control their high LDL blood cholesterol level is to continue taking cholesterol-lowering medications. In short, what is missing is a clear understanding of the factors underlying the elevation of blood cholesterol—largely grains and grain-flour products containing large amounts of glucose they are consuming. Did you know that 100 grams of whole grain contains 77 grams of glucose? In effect, eating a sandwich, a slice of pizza, a doughnut or muffin, and so on—even if it is made with whole grain—floods your body with glucose that, if not used immediately by your muscles and organs, ends up getting stored as fat or raising your cholesterol level.

- Most people do not understand food labels. Canned goods, deli meats, and frozen products often contain voluminous amounts of sodium, far past the daily requirement. When there is an elevation of sodium content in the blood, the body starts to retain more water to keep the sodium concentration within physiological limits. The immediate effect of increased blood volume is elevated blood pressure. Thus, when the heart beats, in order to pump blood out, it has to generate pressure higher than the prevailing pressure in the circulation. The higher the blood pressure, the higher the strain on the heart. Ultimately this could lead to heart failure. Control of blood volume through reduced sodium intake is one thing everyone can do to avoid unnecessary medical management of high blood pressure.

CHAPTER 6

STRATEGIES TO PREVENT DMMI FROM INFLUENCING YOUR HEALTH DECISIONS

IN AN AGE when we are exposed to almost constant and often chaotic information, the power of true information in preventing poor lifestyle conditions cannot be overestimated. In this chapter, I will walk you through a number of strategies you can employ to ensure that you are not a victim of DMMI in making decisions about your health. Most of the advice I am about to give you applies to all of the lifestyle health conditions discussed in this book. However, preventing yourself from becoming ill during a pandemic differs from diabetes, obesity, cancer, and cardiovascular disease. I must therefore start by discussing pandemics separately from those other lifestyle conditions.

Part 1: Pandemics

It has been established that nearly 75% of all new, emerging, or re-emerging diseases affecting humans at the beginning of the 21st century are diseases that normally exist in animals but can jump to humans. Commonly known examples of such diseases are salmonella, malaria, Lyme disease, and the most recent pandemic of the disease called Covid-19, caused by the novel coronavirus SARS-CoV-2.

How do diseases jump from animals to humans? A pathogen such as bacteria, parasite, or virus might be consumed by someone, such as happens with salmonella. The pathogen can be passed through an insect bite, such as a mosquito with malaria. Or the pathogen can be inhaled from air droplets breathed out by the animal, such as with the novel coronavirus.

Although the risks of diseases from animals exist everywhere, they are higher in the tropics where increasing human populations are living in closer proximity to pathogen-rich forests. Impoverished people looking for food and resources to support their families, or humans creating more pathways through the forests for adventure or work, will invariably increase the closeness of humans to animals. This creates greater opportunities for transmission.

For example, coronaviruses are all around us in many animals, from ground-dwelling rodents to tree-dwelling bats. About 24 new coronaviruses have been identified in bats, including four closely related to the virus that causes Covid-19. This is significant in and of itself because bats make about 25 percent of all animal species on earth. However, there are likely to be many more coronaviruses in other animals and in other parts of the world—and one of these may be the cause of the next pandemic.

There is no question about the serious health impact of Covid-19. In the United States, by December 2021 more than 830,000 lives have been lost to the pandemic, with an estimated financial cost of $16 trillion. Unless we are vigilant, the impact of future pandemics could be even worse, perhaps as deadly as the 1918 influenza pandemic which killed 50 million people worldwide. It is estimated that if we suffered a pandemic similar to that of Covid-19 every two decades, the annualized cost would exceed $500 billion per year. Thanks to prior advances in vaccine research and genomic sequencing, among other things such as worldwide cooperation between researchers, we were fortunate that scientists could design vaccines within months of figuring out the genetic code of the coronavirus and that these vaccines appear to be effective even against the various strains of Covid-19.

Pandemics Prevention Principles

Can we prevent pandemics? Prevention of a pandemic in humans depends on first understanding the nature of it, specifically how it originates and spreads.

Pandemic Ingredients. An infectious agent capable of jumping from animals to humans; a mechanism to enter a human, and in the case of viruses, to enter living cells, duplicate, and spread to other humans.

Pandemic Evolution. Since we are in the middle of a SARS-CoV-2 (Covid-19) pandemic, I will use coronavirus as an example to illustrate the evolution of pandemics. Experts say SARS-CoV-2 originated in bats. That's also how the coronaviruses behind Middle East Respiratory Syndrome (MERS) and Severe Acute Respiratory Syndrome (SARS) got started. Bats don't actually get sick when they get infected with coronaviruses; they deftly modulate their immune systems to neutralize their harmful effects, tolerate their presence and, keep carrying and shedding them. In addition to harboring a huge variety of coronaviruses, they are also the suspected reservoir for many diseases, including Nipah and Hendra virus infections, Marburg virus disease, and strains of Influenza A virus.

The precise role of bats in conveying SARS-CoV-2 to humans is debated amongst bat experts because coronaviruses residing in bats can't attach themselves to human cells without modification of the spike protein. But research has also shown that the immediate ancestor of SARS-CoV-2 was likely to have originated in a species of bat. One possibility, therefore, is that bats passed this ancestor onto another species, where it evolved to become SARS-CoV-2, and that intermediate host then passed it to humans. For example, molecular detection and virus isolation studies suggested that the pandemic-causing SARS-CoV jumped from traded civets in wet markets to humans and, similar studies suggested that the MERS-CoV infection in humans was transmitted through close contact with infected camels. On the other hand, in more than 40 years since Ebola was discovered, scientists have not been able to identify the animal it came from.

Pandemic Spread. Every cell in the body is an independent living unit capable of controlling the entry of incoming materials, using receptors on the cell wall for screening. The cell receptor can't make value judgements as to the friendly or harmful nature of the molecule that binds to it. Any successful binding creates the necessary recognition for the cell nucleus to allow the molecule to enter.

For example, when the spike protein on the SARS-CoV-2 virus binds to the receptor angiotensin-converting enzyme 2 (ACE2) located on a host cell membrane, the gene controlling the entry of materials activates enzymes that promote virus entry into the cell. A similar protocol is used by other viruses such as HIV, influenza virus, paramyxovirus, and Ebola to gain entry into a cell. The virus allowed in is then duplicated inside the infected cells and released to infect more cells with ACE2 receptors such as those in the lungs, or it is released outside the body either as respiratory droplets or as aerosol in the exhaled air, capable of infecting others in the vicinity. And thus the pandemic spreads.

As various activities increasingly expose humans to the habitats of bats and other animals, disease outbreaks resulting from transmission of bat coronaviruses will continue to occur in the future. This is inevitable despite the fact that direct transmission of bat coronaviruses to humans appears to be rare. Therefore, it is imperative that we map various known and as yet unknown bat coronaviruses to do risk assessment and reveal the potential intermediate hosts that may play an important role in starting the next pandemic that could be even more severe than that caused by Covid-19.

For example, the Wuhan market had 635 stalls selling live animals. It has been reported that around 47,000 wild animals were sold in Wuhan in two years before some of the first Covid-19 cases emerged there. In short, it was a place of close contact among animals, vendors, and shoppers from many regions of China, an ideal ground for virus transmission from animal to human and spread among humans. We have to be vigilant to make sure that there exists a mechanism for immediate reporting and identification of illnesses suffered by both animals and people in such places.

Pandemic Termination. Mutations are an integral part of coronavirus. Most mutations make the virus weaker and they die out. We never hear about them. However, some mutations make them more capable of evading antibodies and the virus survives longer and spreads wider. In other cases, mutations make the virus more dangerous to the host, increasing the severity of the disease and its complications. On occasion, though rare, these two types of mutations happen in one variant so that it not only spreads faster but also causes more damage.

This appears to be what happened with the Delta variant of Covid-19 that soon became the dominant strain around the world. Ordinarily, further mutations would take the virus in one direction or another because no organism can keep on getting stronger and more evasive at the same time. If it gets stronger, it will find it harder to evade antibodies and die out because it can't infect enough hosts. On the other hand, if it develops more ability to evade antibodies, it becomes weaker but lives longer, especially in small pockets around the world. Over time, it can come back because antibody levels in people drop. This then becomes more akin to just another seasonal flu strain, though at least the pandemic ends. For example, after the Delta variant became the most dominant Covid-19 strain in the world, two variants of concern, the Mu and the Omicron, spread quickly because they could evade antibodies created by the Delta variant vaccine. However, both were less virulent than the Delta, making these variants less troublesome.

Pandemic Containment. Knowing that we can't prevent occasional spillover infections from animals to humans, we have to be able to limit the spread using a number of strategies. Some general guidelines are listed below.

- We can study the nature of interaction between the spike protein and ACE2 to identify susceptible intermediate hosts by comparing the biding affinities between ACE2 and the coronavirus in question.
- We could develop antivirus drugs targeting the spike protein, to prevent attachment of the virus concerned.
- One could develop prototype antibodies against the main component of the spike protein of viruses that show pandemic tendencies such as community spread and be ready to mass produce them if needed.
- We could develop pharmaceutical agents that block the attachment between the virus and ACE2 receptors as another therapeutic target. Another target could be to neutralize the activity of the enzyme(s) needed for facilitating entry of the virus into the cell.
- We might develop other drugs that could incorporate themselves into the virus particle and could impede the rate of proliferation of the virus, thus slowing the virus production and spread.
- The most effective strategy to limit the spread of a viral pandemic is to create immunity to the virus in at least 70%-80% of the susceptible population, known as herd immunity. Immunity means activation of the immune system in the body to create antibodies to block the attachment of the virus to cells or reduce the severity of damage. In addition, immune memory cells that could reactivate antibody production during future encounters with the virus are also created as part of the immune response. This eliminates the need to keep fabricating antibodies in the absence of an imminent threat. Otherwise the blood could become overloaded with antibodies created for different infectious agents.

- It is true that immunity could be produced after a natural infection. However, this takes time and results in a lot of suffering and death among people who are infected before herd immunity is reached. On the other hand, we could create herd immunity to a virus faster by exposing recipients to a vaccine representing selected protein part of the virus. Vaccination does not usurp the development of immunity secondary to natural infection; rather it is a preemptive action because the immune response secondary to vaccination uses the same natural mechanisms in an attempt to prevent infection rather than in response to one. The primary benefit is the potential to avoid severe immediate, delayed, or long-lasting complications. Additionally, unlike infection where the quantity or quality of virus entering the body is unpredictable, vaccination has the advantage of being able to control the quality of the antigen, the age-appropriate dosage for adequate response, the number of injections needed for protection, and the safety and expert evaluation of each step. All these could be carried out using well established protocols to ensure public confidence before the vaccine is approved.

Pandemic Lessons. From the beginning of the coronavirus pandemic detected in December 2019 to December 2021, as this book is going to the press, people around the world experienced almost 300 million Covid-19 infections and more than 5 million deaths. The corresponding numbers in the U.S. were 50 million cases and 830,000 deaths. In view of the real possibility that we can't prevent another pandemic, what lessons have learned that could help us with the next one?

It very clear that no one can predict the time or the place of origin of the next pandemic. Similarly, no one can foresee the rate of spread or the exact nature of the ebbs and tides or the regional hot spots that are likely to happen. For example, the Covid-19 pandemic showed surges and slowdowns, and in some areas, surges on top of an existing surge. Early in 2021 there were simultaneous Covid-19 surges in Northern Hemisphere countries such as India, Pakistan, and Nepal along with surges in Southern Hemisphere countries such as Argentina, Paraguay, and Uruguay. In short, no one can predict why or where a pandemic will take hold, for how long, or the severity and speed of spread. So, understanding these variables as much as possible will help us face the next pandemic. One concrete lesson is that the level of vaccination has a tremendous impact on the final outcome in terms of severity and hospitalizations.

The next lesson is understanding how best to use the vaccine in terms of the number of doses, dose spacing, and dosage amount to maximize the immune response. Although influenza vaccine has been around for some time, the expected effectiveness is not more than 60% because of the unpredictability of virus mutation that gives very little time to incorporate the dominant virus strain protein into the vaccine. This may change with the new RNA-based vaccine that could be tweaked fast to produce a booster dose to the existing flu vaccine in case of significant spread of a variant not represented in the original vaccine formula. We also have to find a way to overcome vaccine hesitancy and understand not just how to make vaccines, but also how to administer vaccinations in a timely fashion to the maximum number of eligible persons.

Pandemic Vaccines

Antiviral vaccines can be classified into two broad categories: 1) gene-based vaccines such as live-virus or nucleic acids that promote antigen production by host cells; and 2) protein-based vaccines that include whole inactivated virus or viral proteins in different combinations, manufactured and administered.

The first step in formulating a vaccine is to generate the antigen that induces an immune response. This can be the inactivated pathogen itself or a subunit of it, or the generation of a recombinant protein derived from the pathogen or another method approved for that purpose.

Next, pathogens such as viruses are grown on cells such as chicken fibroblasts. Some are grown in a semi-synthetic medium and propagated on embryonic chicken eggs. The active components are then propagated in animal, bacterial, fungal or plant cells or by making them via chemical reactions and purified to remove contaminations. Vaccine components are then mixed to optimize an effective immune response in the body, remain stable, and be produced at scale. A vaccine is then packaged in syringes, vials, or other containers, then labelled and packaged for shipment. Frequent sampling and testing throughout the manufacturing process ensures consistency and microbiological integrity.

Usually, vaccine development takes years if not decades before they can be approved and available for large-scale distribution. However, the coronavirus vaccine production was speeded up because of new tools such as structure-based antigen design, protein engineering, new manufacturing platforms, and other discoveries to make the production occur with speed and precision. For example, scientists have been studying mRNA vaccines for flu, Zika, rabies and cytomegalovirus. This work provided the necessary information to design the Covid-19 mRNA vaccine faster than any other vaccine in the past.

Yet another positive development was the Spike Ferritin Nanoparticle (SpFN) COVID-19 vaccine or the Spike Receptor-Binding Domain Ferritin Nanoparticle (RFN) vaccine, which targets a smaller part of the coronavirus spike protein than the SpFN vaccine, both developed by researchers at the Walter Reed Army Institute of Research (WRAIR). These types of vaccines not only elicit a potent immune response but may also provide broad protection against SARS-CoV-2 variants as well as other coronaviruses.

The Novavax vaccine and the GlaxoSmithKline/Sanofi Pasteur vaccine contain part of the spike protein of SARS-CoV-2 to trigger an immune response. The AstraZeneca/University of Oxford vaccine contains a harmless weakened adenovirus that has been modified to include the genetic information of the SARS-CoV-2 surface Spike protein.

The Pfizer/BioNTech vaccine and the Moderna vaccines are the first ever RNA-based vaccines to be approved for use in humans. They contain the genetic information needed to build the SARS-CoV-2 spike protein. RNA-based vaccines can be produced using chemical processes that don't require a cell culture system or high-level biosafety containment, making their manufacture faster and easier than for other types of vaccines. This process can be adapted to produce vaccines based on coronavirus variants that may not be blocked by antibodies produced using existing antigens.

Yet another potential source of vaccine, as reported by a Canadian biotech firm, is the development of viral vaccines in plants related to tobacco. A prototype Covid vaccine showed 70%-78% efficacy to prevent moderate and severe disease, according to the company. One advantage of this vaccine is it does not need special freezers to store it. Standard refrigeration is adequate. [footnote number for end of book]

Careful evaluation of vaccines in healthy adults in conjunction with studies in animal models can accelerate Covid-19 vaccine development. For example, animals such as pangolins, dogs, cats, hamsters, voles, lemmings, and muskrats have shown susceptibility to coronaviruses and could be targets for carefully supervised laboratory studies for discovering reliable vaccine design as well as for testing effective antiviral therapeutics. Pre-planning process development to scale-up production capacity along with timely development of distribution and administration strategies can speed vaccine availability.[20]

Preparing for Future Pandemics

Unless we are vigilant, the impact of future pandemics could be even worse, perhaps as deadly as the 1918 influenza pandemic which killed 50 million people worldwide. It is estimated that if we suffered a pandemic similar to that of Covid-19 every two decades, the annualized cost would exceed $500 billion per year.

To protect lives and prevent financial ruin, the U.S. needs a comprehensive and detailed plan to prepare the nation for the next pandemic. The following strategies are offered to ensure that our political leaders and health officials who have a responsibility to protect citizens from a deadly virus are prepared.

1. Keep track of potential pathogens. Prevention of a pandemic is easier if we can identify potential pathogens and their mode of entry before they get into the human body. In March 2021, more than two dozen world leaders proposed such a framework on pandemic preparedness and response. I suggest that we need an International Repository for reporting all infections contracted by people who routinely work with animals, be it in farms, zoos, animal care facilities, or veterinary offices. This type of cooperation will help us identify and track any genomic variances from the original to one that could efficiently spread to humans and then among humans. To control the spread, we must be able to know about the origin of the agent, its mutations and its transmissibility.

2. Quickly identify viruses. When community spread occurs, meaning when the virus is passed on to others by a person with no symptoms, the CDC and/or WHO should send a team immediately to identify the virus and assess its potential for spread. This suggestion is no different than what occurs now in the U.S, Department of Justice, which currently uses Facial Recognition Technology to react quickly and effectively to emerging threats. Imagine the benefit if we can develop a similar technology based on the structural characteristics of a pathogen for real-time identification. Research that normally might take days or weeks to identify the genomic sequence, by combing through databases and other information already available to scientists, could instead be accomplished in a very short time period. In the case of viral pathogens, the database can be the depository of information related to specific characteristics of the mechanism each virus uses to attach itself to the cell wall to gain entry into a cell. In fact, with adequate resources, we could even create a catalogue of prototype vaccines against those viruses considered capable of starting a pandemic.

3. Develop a reliable test. We need accurate validated test kits that are widely distributed as soon as possible. Test and monitor as many contacts as possible to understand the mechanism and speed of spread. This will also reveal whether the infection's impact is mild, moderate, or serious and the necessity for isolation, contact tracing and quarantine.

Covid-19 spread quickly in the U.S. in part because of a failure to make and distribute accurate testing kits around the country. To make matters worse, President Trump also insisted that little testing be done, based on his false theory that more testing creates more cases, as if the infections would not be there without the testing. The virus was a potentially containable outbreak before spreading rapidly across the globe. In contrast, there are many viral outbreaks every year that are controlled before they become epidemics. For example, Uganda in 2018 prevented the Ebola epidemic by quickly activating its national emergency preparedness and response systems, training healthcare staff, opening up multiple centers for rapid testing and treating, as well as screening visitors entering the country.

4. Develop a vaccine using the latest technologies and have a clear plan to vaccinate the most vulnerable. Having a national vaccination plan in advance can go a long way to minimizing the spread of the virus. It is true that experts may not be sure, especially in the early stages of vaccine production when vaccine supply is limited, who should be prioritized first to receive it—those who are most likely to spread the virus versus those who might be most vulnerable to dying from it. The United States prioritized older people because they were most likely to die from the Covid-19 infection. The fast emergence of new Covid variants, such as Delta, highlights the importance of having reprogrammable vaccines that can be tweaked to match the new virus model and the need for detailed planning.

5. Public service messaging to promote vaccination. The U.S. is currently undergoing a 4th wave of Covid-19, largely because nearly 50% of eligible people are unable or refusing to be vaccinated. The science of pandemic spread has become politicized, largely according to "red" (Republican) states that have politicians who promote disinformation about vaccines versus "blue" (Democratic) states where the politicians have endorsed the critical need to be vaccinated. This politicization and polarization of science has not happened before with this high level of divisiveness.

When the polio vaccine became available in the 1950s, the March of Dimes helped with advertising on posters featuring young children who were most at risk of being infected. Public figures were actively recruited to promote the vaccine. For example, Elvis Presly got vaccinated right on the popular, highly watched television program *The Ed Sullivan Show*. In contrast, former President Donald J. Trump, despite having helped facilitate the rapid production of vaccines in record time, has never used his influence to convince his own base of followers, let alone the country, to get the vaccine. In fact, he got vaccinated in private before leaving the White House and has never offered to do any public service announcements (PSAs) to endorse vaccinations.

It is to be noted that mistakes may have been made in the messaging about vaccines when Trump first announced the efforts to produce the vaccines quickly. Debra Furr-Holden, associate dean for public health integration at Michigan State University, attributed at least some of the vaccination resistance to communications failures, starting with the branding of "Operation Warp Speed," the federal effort to develop a coronavirus vaccine quickly. "When people heard 'warp speed,' you know what they heard? Corner cutting, skipped steps, missed steps, quick and dirty," she said. In her opinion, the United States should have launched a mass literacy campaign on vaccines long before they were produced and made it far easier to get vaccinated once shots were available. "We should be vaccinating people on their front doorsteps," she said.

In the first seven months after the vaccines became available in the U.S., it was given to those in the most vulnerable age groups and to first responders. This was to be expected; the Food and Drug Administration and the Centers for Disease Control and Prevention had to stick to strict scientific and medical opinions to issue clear guidelines about vaccination priorities, and then to modify them as new data were collected. When the rate of vaccine administration slowed after several months, the message was then retargeted towards the reluctant. Some states offered lotteries with prizes and most local governments made accessibility easier for anyone interested in receiving the vaccine.

Yet, by the summer of 2021, it was evident that 90 million Americans who could have received the shot were still unvaccinated, a majority of those people for personal and political reasons rather than sincere health doubts or concerns. Other factors apply as well; according to a U.S. census survey released in July 2021, among Americans eligible and *willing* to get vaccinated, the higher a person's household income, the more likely the person was to have received a shot. However, among those who *refused* to accept the vaccines, people who self-identified as Republican were in the majority.

Researchers at the University of Texas at Austin have suggested that many more lives could have been saved by targeting vaccine messages to the ZIP codes hardest-hit by Covid-19. The lessons here are that the adverse political and anti-science social environments may demand more interventions from local and state leaders and even private businesses. However, we must be careful about this strategy; determining the best practices for the safety of the public more by geography and the whims of politicians than by relying on the science could result in a disaster in containing a future pandemic.

6. Use data to model how to control the pandemic. Model the potential strategies to minimize a pandemic using data about equipment, medical supplies, number and type of caregivers, and other facilities that would be needed for messaging and to administer vaccines. Historically, vaccines have taken years to develop. For example, the mumps vaccine, the fastest vaccine to be approved for use in humans at the time, took four years to develop. However, we now know that with the newest technologies, plans can be in place to acquire necessary agents, equipment, facilities, and personnel not only for the production and distribution of vaccines but also for dissemination of preventive measures and administration of the vaccination process. In addition, we must fund new research focused on finding safe and effective therapies and cures that directly destroy viruses or at least slow viral replication. Although this may not be faster or more accurate than vaccines that prepare the immune system to prevent infection, this could be acceptable even by those who may not be willing to take the vaccine. Equally important is collecting data on long-term impact of the pandemic on children.

7. Promote personal care measures. We also must use every available system to alert the public to the importance of personal care measures to prevent the spread of the infectious agent to the level of a pandemic. For example, hand washing, mask wearing, and social distancing should be taught as part of a wellness plan in all schools and workplaces. Social media should especially be used to tell the truth about personal care and to disallow DMMI from infiltrating their airwaves. Closing schools, theaters, and even places of worship, limiting public transportation, and banning large public gatherings could significantly reduce the strain on the healthcare system that at some point simply cannot care for thousands of people who need acute critical care. These measures need to be promoted as necessary at the beginning of viral spread, rather than promoted as something extreme and dangerous.

8. Ongoing surveillance of virus mutations. The process of "coevolution" between an infectious agent and a host can lead to hosts becoming resistant to the agent (which is useful), but it can also lead to the agent developing greater virulence to attack the host (which is very bad). The scientific methodology that identifies mutations in a virus, and its further transmissibility to animals, children, and adults (such as a propensity for airborne spread or for increased attachment time) and its increased lethality is called surveillance. Ongoing surveillance makes it possible to detect mutations that might change the behavior of the virus at the earliest recognition of them, so that health authorities can take appropriate action to contain the mutated virus. Surveillance also allows authorities to reevaluate the specificity and sensitivity of testing kits, and the effectiveness of antibodies, natural as well as vaccine induced.

9. Free or inexpensive access to health information and care. Everyone should have affordable or free access to reliable information and healthcare related to pandemics. Otherwise the pandemic will be prolonged because of a reservoir of infected people in the community who cannot obtain care. Special efforts may be needed to reach all those who are immunocompromised, on immunosuppressive treatments, and those with autoimmune disease. Even those who have been immunized need to know whether they could still carry the virus and spread it to others—through breakthrough infection and asymptomatic spread—despite not experiencing any symptoms of being infected.

It is especially important for the general public to understand the potential for a virus to mutate if given a chance to replicate. A new version of the virus could be more efficient in multiplying faster, staying in the air longer, or evading the antibodies, either produced in response to natural infection or through vaccination. The lack of understanding of this issue may be one reason why the Delta variant has spread so quickly and widely in the U.S in the summer of 2021.

10. Combat resistance to the government's and health authorities' preventive measures. It is absolutely clear from the spread of Covid-19 that we cannot tolerate any infiltration of DMMI, such as that which has been so prevalent due to the massive volume of anti-science and anti-vaccination messaging, largely from right-wing media, that irrationally claims to be protecting personal freedoms. There is no freedom for the more than 830,000 who have died and the nearly 50 million who have been infected (some with long-term consequences). It is vital that leaders be empathic, educated, and trustworthy, so that their messages regarding preventive measures are not resisted by the general public.

Those who reject vaccinations are endangering the freedom (and lives) of everyone else. One's personal freedom does not extend to having the freedom to infect other people. Countries such as Taiwan, Singapore, and Hong Kong took rapid action against Covid-19, based upon lessons drawn from earlier outbreaks. Those nations have demonstrated beyond any doubt that the trajectory of an outbreak can be altered with organized, sustained, science-based and accurate messaging, timely testing, improved health systems, and determined leadership.

Part 2: Lifestyle Conditions

The kind of information you rely on to make choices about your health and lifestyle is critical. DMMI—Disinformation, Misinformation, and Missing Information—contributes to unfortunate decision-making that can lead to diabetes, cardiovascular disease, or cancer. On the other hand, accurate information leads to decisions that can affect your health in positive ways. Here are my suggestions for how to learn the truth and avoid DMMI.

1. Evaluate the Message for Logic, Mechanism, and Evidence

When a practitioner is confronted with a medical condition, he or she is encouraged to ask, is the condition caused by the *presence* of an agent (a virus, bacteria, etc.), or the result of the *absence* of an agent (a natural hormone, vitamin, enzyme that might be missing)? This is good advice for everyone. Before accepting any information related to the cause or treatment of lifestyle conditions as true, stop and analyze whether the information clearly demonstrates a logic, has a mechanism, and is based on evidence. Look for the answers to these questions:

- Logic: Does the information presented make sense in the context of the condition?
- Mechanism: Has a clear, understandable mechanism been explained and accepted?
- Evidence: Is there evidence (of the cause and/or a treatment benefit) based on controlled studies?

Every explanation of how a medical illness or condition occurs needs to fulfill these requirements to be acceptable. Consider this example about medications that claim to help with Type 2 diabetes. Many pharmaceutical companies advertise products designed to lower blood glucose level. The public's repeated exposure to such advertisements leads to the impression that by lowering blood glucose level using that medication, they can prevent diabetic complications. Medical practitioners, when asked for evidence proving that the drug prevents diabetic complications, tend to point to the statistics regarding how the medicine lowers blood glucose levels, just as advertised. In doing this, they are making a circular argument, using the proof of lowering glucose as the evidence for the decreased complications. This is not how logic works. Instead, what the evidence should prove is that lowered glucose decreases complications.

Another example of the importance of scrutinizing the logic used by a source of information or its lack of evidence is in the area of side effects. When you encounter arguments claiming that a medication has "side effects," that could often be a way of wording the fact that the medicine's "side effects" are actually responsible for the observed "benefit."

For instance, metformin is commonly used in early diagnosed Type 2 diabetes patients. But metformin produces more gastrointestinal symptoms (range: 2% to 63%) than most other oral diabetes agents (range: 0% to 32% for second-generation sulfonylureas). The most common adverse effects include diarrhea, nausea, and abdominal pain. These all can significantly impact the patient's food intake and thus result in a lower blood glucose level.

There is no evidence that metformin researchers excluded in their data people who experienced adverse gastrointestinal effects. Rather, researchers concluded that metformin was an effective oral agent for the treatment of Type 2 diabetes. The missing information is how metformin actually lowers blood glucose on its own. In my opinion, the medication appears to work because so many people on metformin have digestive problems that force reduced food intake, which in turn lowers their blood glucose.

I would endorse metformin if the investigators can actually show a mechanism by which the drug overcomes the supposed insulin resistance, or facilitates entry of glucose into specific cells, or demonstrates a true long-term reduction in the incidence of associated complications as a result of metformin therapy. Increased peripheral glucose uptake and reduced output of glucose from the liver have been suggested to explain how patients on metformin lower blood glucose levels. But no research has been presented to explain how metformin accomplishes these.

Another example: Improper diet and lack of exercise are often promoted as causes of cancer. However, there is seldom a validated explanation of how this happens with full proof of the logic, mechanism, and evidence for the reasoning.

Even the Best Medical Research Can Contain Errors

You probably don't read professional medical research, but you should know that it is not always right. Scientific research can be very difficult to perform and to analyze with conclusive results. Researchers may do their best but they do make mistakes, misjudgments, and incorrect analyses. Sometimes, even conclusions presented in articles published in respected medical journals may not be valid. The way science works often obscures the truth about the real value of some of the recommendations. In short, there could be potential problems with every type of medical study, as explained below:

Prospective studies: These are studies done after approval by an accredited agency of an institution or government after reviewing the study protocol regarding participants, data collection, and data analysis. Each of these is a potential area for mistakes to occur. In addition, there can be problems associated with the use of a technique for statistical analysis that is actually not appropriate for the study. Statistical analyses are sometimes chosen to produce the result desired by the sponsor of the study. Even more troubling is the motivation of each participant. For example, during one of my studies, I discovered that one participant fabricated the results, because he wanted to please me by obtaining the results he thought I was looking for.

Retrospective studies: These are studies using data gathered from existing documents or from the recollections of participants. These studies are notoriously unreliable because of errors in the original documentation and recollection. You can imagine that a study that collates evidence from many studies can only be accurate and correct if all of the collated studies were correct.

Associative studies: These studies show results when one particular parameter can be associated with a particular result. For example, there are studies that seek to show that the frequency or quantity of drinking alcohol can be correlated to the incidence of cancer. Another study, the Framingham Offspring Study, analyzed the eating patterns of people diagnosed with gastroesophageal cancer. Although such studies can be used to relate general drinking and eating patterns with well-being or disease status, to completely understand the cause and effect relationship, one needs to consider a wide array of possible combinations of dietary components. Even then, the results may not offer an absolutely accurate answer because of intentional and unintentional errors in reporting by subjects, unknown interactions between two or more elements, and the variability of metabolism and genetic responses within each individual. In other words, to use a common warning regarding potential errors in logic: "correlation does not prove causation."

The conclusions in such studies could be tainted by a lack of reliable data or by the omission of other factors that might be better correlated, such as genetic susceptibility, viral infections, smoking, etc.

2. Evaluate the Messenger

The second strategy that you need to employ in your quest to detect DMMI is to evaluate the messenger who is delivering the information to the public. You may have heard this expressed as "consider the source." The problem is, humans are selective in what we decide to accept as true. In our quest for accurate information, humans are programmed to ignore most of that which we don't agree with. Otherwise we would be experiencing a lot more stress. There is enough stress already in trying to get a clear understanding of information that we agree with.

It is hard not to believe a leader who has been found to be correct often enough. However, when it comes to your health needs, I suggest that you consider the following before blindly following the leader's recommendations, especially if the leader does not have the capability or training to clearly understand what he or she is promoting. For example, when discussing pandemics, diabetes, cancer, or cardiovascular disease, does the leader have any background or education in those areas? If not trained in health sciences, where did the leader get the information from? Often, the leader depends on a trustworthy source before advocating a position regarding a health recommendation. However, the expert advising the leader could shade the message to fit the outcome desired by the leader.

Similarly, does the presenter exaggerate a claim or fail to clarify exactly what a medication or supplement does? For example, if the promotion is for a product that enhances memory, is the enhancement limited to short-term memory or is it about long-term memory? Or, if the product is for boosting the immune system, does the presenter discuss whether it can worsen an autoimmune illness?

In short, you have to keep in mind that any supposedly reliable source that you have come to accept may not be reliable at all times. They could occasionally represent vested interests that are promulgating one or more forms of DMMI. By recognizing this, and keeping it in mind as you read articles, watch TV, skim the social media, and talk to others, you might choose to revise your assessment of that information. It is important to try and determine if the messenger has had the necessary training and time to evaluate the product or service they are promoting, or are they likely to be doing so in exchange for compensation or as a favor?

Here is another example. You may prefer either progressive or conservative media and tend to agree with their take on an economic or foreign policy story. Often different "sides" of an issue agree on the ultimate goal but differ on the methods for achieving that goal. And that kind of difference of opinion is fine. But when it comes to medical information such as facts about Covid-19, the current conservative media has promoted many scientifically incorrect stories about the virus and how to protect oneself and the general population from it. It seems the conservative media has politicized the truth about vaccines and masking, for instance. They denigrate and object to public health measures such as proof of vaccination and masking by characterizing those requirements as an infringement on personal liberty. They imply, or even come right out and state, that the U.S. has never imposed such public health measures in the past or that the current government is stepping far beyond the boundaries of what the Constitution allows.

But historically, there have been many other instances of required public health measures in the United States. Consider the practice of quarantining; for instance, it was required by the 1647 quarantine law in the Massachusetts colony, and there were mass quarantines of immigrants entering the country in the 19th-century. The 1905 Supreme Court decision upholding compulsory vaccination to halt a smallpox epidemic is another example. When the polio vaccine was invented, few people refused to take it, because its efficacy was undeniable and the need for it was clear and unquestioned. The same has been true (efficacy and necessity) for the major American-produced Covid-19 vaccines, but still a significant percentage of people refuse to be vaccinated due to the DMMI about them on conservative news outlets.

Arguments that public health measures violate our liberties are short-sighted and illogical arguments. If people refuse to get vaccinated or wear masks, it is clear they are more likely to spread the virus. The more the virus spreads, the more people become sick, hospitalized, or even die as we are now seeing throughout the "red" states in the South, where the Delta variant is returning the country to case and death statistics higher than the initial spread of the pandemic. All the people who became infected by those who refuse vaccination or masks under the rubric of personal liberty suffer having *their* personal freedom infringed upon. Then as time goes on, and even more people become sick, the pandemic continues to spread, making it dangerous for nearly everyone to conduct their daily life.

As this most recent wave of the pandemic spreads, the risks of disease could easily become so great that agencies at all levels of government—federal, state, and local—could once again determine that it is necessary to close businesses, schools, and public gatherings. *Everyone's* freedom is now jeopardized because of the few who claimed initially and erroneously that vaccinations and wearing masks are infringements on *their* freedom.

There is simply no logic to such "violation of freedom" arguments, when the Constitution is based on creating a democratic society that protects everyone's rights. No one seems to complain that they should be allowed to drive the wrong way down a one-way street because "personal freedom" guarantees it. No one insists it is a violation of their personal freedom that they cannot concoct some home brew in their kitchen and go out and sell it as a cancer cure on the street. It is not a violation of freedom to issue public health guidelines that seek to prevent one person from infecting other people with a deadly virus.

The point is, it is easy to blindly follow information coming from a source that you have come to trust. But periodically, you need to evaluate your source and confirm that they are actually telling the truth, not disseminating disinformation or misinformation. This is especially vital when the information concerns a lifestyle condition you are dealing with and which is critical to your health and well-being.

If you are willing to evaluate the messenger, consider these suggestions:

- **Examine the personality of the presenter**. You are likely to follow the opinions presented by someone with great communication skills, but that does not mean the person is providing accurate information. They may appear to be very sympathetic to the ideology you have come to believe in, but they may also have ulterior motives such as politics, personal fame, or greed. Beware especially of people with autocratic tendencies. They are likely to ignore that which they do not understand and therefore they fail to take that evidence into consideration when promoting a solution, product, or procedure.

- **Look for patterns of DMMI from the presenter.** Does the presenter have a pattern of disinformation, misinformation, or not fully explaining the problem when he or she deals with issues unrelated to health? If so, be careful before fully following health-related instructions they may issue. Your bias to accept the presenter when it comes to health-related issues might change if you recognize that the presenter is promoting DMMI in other areas.
- **Check to see if the presenter insists on always being right.** Is there evidence that the presenter admits to making a mistake or apologizes to someone who has presented evidence contrary to that of the presenter? If so, the presenter is likely to be an honest person. But if the presenter comes across as always being right, without ever acknowledging they might be wrong or do not know something, it is a sign that he or she is unwilling to be objective about what the truth is. If they refuse any discussion or debate, take that as a red flag.
- **Evaluate if the presenter seeks to create confusion and relies on Scripture rather than science.** Does the presenter use symbolism associated with the devil, blame others, or call them evil in an attempt to prove that opinions contrary to theirs must be wrong? Does the presenter rely on religious arguments to oppose scientific arguments? When it comes to pandemics, diabetes, cancer, and heart disease, there is little proof that any belief system has been able to keep even the most dedicated believers from dying. There may be some instances of miraculous cures for which science may not have a clear explanation. But we must accept that most people—even children—are not saved from debilitating illness and ultimate death through prayer or belief in God alone, but rather through sound medical treatment when possible. (One could argue that the way

God works is actually by providing us with dedicated scientists and effective vaccines and treatments.)

- **Check if the presenter uses selective associations as evidence.** Some presenters will take a single positive element of the results from a study while ignoring the negatives from the same study. Or they might use a negative element to discredit a differing opinion, while ignoring the positives associated with the recommendation. Similarly, does the promoter discredit the opinion of an opposing presenter by using it out of context? Some memes on social media are especially dangerous because they do just this.

3. Evaluate what you see on websites and social media, where disinformation and misinformation are rampant.

The internet can be a forum to inform, entertain, and share. It can be an invaluable tool to reach people who might be immediately affected by incoming inclement weather or other natural calamities; to provide information about blocked or diverted transportation systems; to inform the public about missing persons or dangerous escapees from a correctional facility; as a conduit to collect money for charities, business ventures, political, religious or other organizations; and to convey holiday greetings, birthday wishes, and get-well messages. It could be a platform to summon help in an instant on an important need.

But websites and social media can also be the source of substantial disinformation and misinformation, promoted by people with vested interests, by criminals and malicious actors, by foreign agents attempting to sow discord in this country, and by adults and kids just playing on people's gullibility.

One problem is that social media thrives on "hits," "clicks," and page views, making it desirable to create postings and advertising to earn money. This tends to reward contentious content that feeds into people's prejudices, political anger, and stereotypes; people love to read postings and tweets that reinforce their beliefs. This is also true of postings and tweets about unhealthy behaviors, easy fixes, and fake remedies as people search for ways to solve their problems easily and cheaply.

A simple posting that claims to have "An easy way to lose weight," or "A food supplement to reverse your diabetes" may not have a shred of scientific evidence in it but can become very popular, generating millions of clicks and thousands of believers. The same goes for a posting or tweet that claims to have evidence that vaccines are harmful or that children wearing masks at school will suffer psychological damage and asking them to do so is an invasion of parental rights.

With the well-established and critical importance of social media, how might we figure out how to screen information for reliability and authenticity rather than by how many people are looking at it? At this time, the problem of controlling rampant disinformation and misinformation on social media presents a myriad of difficult challenges. Consider these questions that point out the dilemma we face:

1. Can we expect social media companies to do truth screening for us?
2. How can we curtail the spread of disinformation and misinformation when there are monetary incentives that drive posting them?
3. Can we hold a social media outlet responsible for someone putting illegal content on it?
4. Who should be in charge of regulating online speech, without stifling online communications and while at the same time allowing businesses to benefit?
5. How can we determine if any harm that occurred to someone was because he or she did not clearly understand the message or voluntarily believed it? Can the person posting a falsehood be blamed for that?

Attempts to eliminate disinformation and misinformation from the internet and social media often appear to impinge on freedom of speech, which is enshrined in our Constitution. It is politically challenging to put limits on free speech, but equally important to prevent fake news from taking over the internet and social media.

Nevertheless, as a civilized society, we must begin taking actions to limit the spread of disinformation and misinformation, especially when it relates to the public's health. Only with the spread of accurate and true information can we expect to change public consciousness about the destructive risks of false information. There is too much at stake in the world for people to be misled about protecting their health. The advent of telemedicine has made it possible for both accredited experts as well those who present themselves as experts to offer advice related to almost any illness to anyone looking for it, regardless of the location of the seeker or the expert.

When using the internet and social media, it is important to develop the habit of being constantly on your guard for disinformation and misinformation. Recognize that social media is rampant with fake news postings, false or exaggerated claims, and planted disinformation from many. We know that some elements of the conservative media are especially intent on using anti-science and fake news about Covid-19, vaccines, and masking. Whether you tend to agree with the conservative news media on economic matters, domestic planning, and foreign policy, you should also be aware that believing the reams of medical disinformation and misinformation that many conservative news stations and social media sites pump out carries a different set of repercussions.

Given the known rampant volume of disinformation and misinformation on the internet and social media, one must approach medical- and health-related information with some skepticism. You must ask yourself, does this make logical sense? Does it jive with what you already know about science? Does it reflect a "conspiracy" theory that goes against logic and all evidence (such as that Bill Gates planted microchips into the vaccines to monitor your movements)? Does it propose a seemingly simple solution to a complex problem, which often means the source has not considered all the factors and is neglecting other evidence?

Especially check to see if the information comes from a source that has a vested interest in selling you a product. For example, getting timely information regarding the functional competency of an organ or system in the body while undergoing a test, procedure, or treatment and follow-up thereafter is invaluable. Gadgets already on the market and/or being developed make it possible for continuous monitoring of almost every organ or system in one form or another. But beware: with the clever use of social media, pharmaceutical companies and gadget makers can try to convince people that by obtaining health information with their products, they are somehow in a better position to protect their health compared to those who do not use such means. This, in turn, would embolden the purveyors of these products to exaggerate the importance and utility of these devices to convince the vulnerable that without these gadgets, they are putting their health in danger, especially if they can afford it. While many could interpret the data from these gadgets and act on it in a beneficial way, many others could get anxious by anticipating bad outcomes or, worse, try unproven remedies to prevent an imaginary worsening of an existing medical condition.

And finally, ask yourself, if you know others who have followed that information or advice, is there evidence that they are alive and thriving in great health? The news is full of reports of people who declined to get vaccinated becoming ill with Covid-19, with many of them dying. At this time, 99% of patients who die from Covid-19 in many states are people who refused to get vaccinated, so it would be illogical to take chances and continue to remain unvaccinated, despite what many social media postings suggest. Similarly, many people believe that treatment with laetrile can cure their cancer. They may find postings and tweets touting laetrile, but nearly every report of scientific evidence does not support such claims.

In short, I suggest that postings on social media are more likely to mislead you when it comes to providing accurate, science-based information about the health conditions covered in this book: pandemics, Type 2 diabetes, cancer, and cardiovascular disease.

Which is Better: Vaccination or Natural Infection?

One of the most challenging components of chaotic information is the one that starts with solid scientific evidence but then veers into advocating a preferred point of view without giving more facts that could allow the reader to make informed decisions. A case in point is the recent debate often seen on social media over protection from reinfection related to Covid-19 vaccine versus natural infection. Some people are posting on many social media sites that it is equally or more effective to get infected to develop immunity against Covid-19 rather than get the vaccine. This is not true—and the tipoff is that is seldom backed up by scientific evidence.

Recall that there are two arms to natural immunity, with antibodies providing short-term protection and memory cells providing long-term protection from reinfection. Currently, there are no tests to measure the number of memory cells created either from natural infection or from vaccination. On the other hand, tests show robust antibody production both from natural infection and from vaccination. This can be used by some to suggest that developing antibodies in response to an infection is a superior mechanism because it is more natural compared to antibodies produced in response to vaccination.

The problem here is that there is no reliable way to compare the protective effect of antibodies produced in either of these situations because antibody levels tapper off over time, regardless of the trigger that led to their production. Secondly, even when the total antibody level is similar, the effectiveness of infection prevention can be variable. This happens because, during an infection, the immune system can produce antibodies to different parts of the virus, whereas antibodies produced after Covid-mRNA vaccination are more targeted to block viral attachment. Therefore, unit for unit, you are likely to get more protection from vaccination-induced antibodies than from those produced during a natural infection.

Also, different variants of Covid-19 produce different types of immune response. In addition, if you are hospitalized with Covid-19, you are likely to have a better immune response compared to that produced by an asymptomatic mild infection. On the other hand, as mentioned, antibodies after mRNA vaccine are more specific. In fact, a CDC study published in August suggested people who got Covid-19 in 2020 and didn't get a vaccine were more than twice as likely to be reinfected in May or June 2021 when compared with people who also had Covid-19 but were later fully vaccinated.[21]

However, many people may not be aware that the main reason to be vaccinated rather than get the infection would be to avoid the possibility of severe complications, including death, from a natural infection.

4. Promote universal efforts to rid the world of disinformation and misinformation.

I suggest that the public also needs to stand behind efforts to eliminate false information.

This can start first at the community level. We need community health communication programs that address health-related issues in underserved areas and neighborhoods experiencing the highest health illiteracy rates. These could be patterned after the REDI (Rapid Employment and Development Initiative) started after a 2016 spike in gun violence in Chicago. Evaluation of the effectiveness of the initiative two years after its intensive coaching showed that the participants were less likely to be victims of gun homicide or shootings. We need a similar program that helps increase the health literacy of people who suffer from the highest cases of lifestyle illnesses such as obesity, Type 2 diabetes, cancer, and cardiovascular disease.

At a higher level, I believe the time has also come for an international accord to prevent the unforeseen from becoming a reality. By that I am referring to a situation whereby we end up with a critical mass of people driven by ideology promoted by influential leaders cause the internet and social media to become a tool to promulgate propaganda—the most extreme form of disinformation and misinformation. The continued evolution of new technology and its applications demand that we begin developing this international accord immediately so the world can begin to cut off the increasing volume of fake news.

In his classic 1946 essay, "Politics and the English Language," the English writer George Orwell wrote, "Political language—and with variations this is true of all political parties, from Conservatives to Anarchists—is designed to make falsehoods sound truthful and murder respectable, and to give an appearance of solidity to pure wind." This means that influential groups with vested interests or a particular mindset can popularize disinformation or misinformation to the public, hiding behind the idea that they are simply supporting the "open dissemination" of information, such that a significant number of people may come to believe in the disinformation or misinformation even without understanding it.

We see this happening with the entire anti-vaccination movement in which a small number of people have warped the scientific proof about vaccines and are continuously spreading vast quantities of disinformation that many others have come to accept as true. They neglect to point out actual facts about the history of vaccines, such as how smallpox was eradicated with a vaccine.

Only clear explanations of a true nature can help change public consciousness so that people know what is at stake and what actions are necessary to protect their health.

However, this still requires a delicate balance and an understanding of the process medical science must follow to discover the true facts. For example, consider what has to happen when a new illness with the potential to become an epidemic (meaning locally spread) or a pandemic (meaning very widespread) is suspected, such as when an observant medical care provider notices a higher than expected incidence of illness due to a pathogen. Before it is identified as an epidemic or pandemic, medical personnel must collect data regarding the cause, the pathways of spread, and possible methods of prevention and treatments.

During this time, an infected person's care provider must take care in how they communicate with the patient and their family. If miscommunication occurs regarding the potential pathogen, it could generate widespread attention through social media, which could have the adverse effect of creating a panic response. Such responses can then have undesired consequences such as the hoarding of food, medicine, gasoline, etc. In addition, if this coincides with an expected private or public event already planned, the news could have devastating economic consequences for the local business community.

Finally, there is no doubt that we need to strengthen our public health system. In a series of studies beginning in the late 1960s and continuing to the present day, Sir Michael Marmot has been pursuing the impact of social, economic, and political determinants upon various populations. Although he primarily focused on Indigenous peoples, his suggestions are applicable to all healthcare systems. For example, he states that healthcare systems need to 1) promote improved education, 2) promote expanded vocational support and improved working conditions, 3) promote healthy living conditions and adequate housing, 4) give every child the best start in life, 5) advocate to establish an income necessary for a healthy life, and 6) pursue the cause of the causes of ill health.

5. Be aware that you might be missing information.

I had great difficulty writing a recommendation for this because how can I communicate to anyone how to identify situations where you may be missing information and therefore likely to be influenced by DMMI that is misleading you into making bad healthcare decisions? This is the perennial dilemma: how do you know what you don't know? When should you assess that you may be missing information before you make a choice about your lifestyle that might lead to a lifestyle condition such as diabetes, cancer, or cardiovascular disease?

I decided to explain it by reflecting on how we learn anything. Learning is the process of filling in gaps in our knowledge or acquiring new information that you find useful or interesting. When an adult looks at an object, the mind tries to search for all previous encounters or knowledge associated with that object stored in memory. In contrast, a child having no previous experience with some topic can form an opinion not affected by a previous encounter.

This means that, unlike adults who make decisions based on analysis, the child's decision is based on whether the encounter is agreeable or disagreeable. A child's brain stores the episode along with the feelings it evoked. After repeated similar encounters, the information gets stored in memory. For example, a child hearing a story for the first time is unable to understand the details of the story. Even after reading or hearing it multiple times, the child still may not completely grasp a social or moral concept embedded in the story. Yet, the excitement created in the brain upon learning creates the curiosity that is necessary for continued learning.

It won't take long for the child to understand that not all encounters in life are pleasing; some are downright unpleasant or even painful. Soon, the child starts developing coping mechanisms such as avoiding encounters that can lead to unpleasantness or trying to minimize the feeling created in the mind by not dwelling on it. As we get older, we then learn that we can plan our lives to expect only happy events; unhappy events thus occur mostly unexpectedly. Many of us take it one step further and try not to look for missing information, especially when it comes to one's own health, because it could be unpleasant.

In addition, even if you are proactive regarding learning about your health, you may not know enough about the health condition to ask the right questions. For example, how would you know that elevated blood sugar can be due either to overconsumption of glucose-containing products or the underutilization of glucose in the body? Without this knowledge, how can you question it when your doctor tells you that you have developed insulin resistance and therefore your blood glucose elevation is secondary to underutilization and must be corrected by medications? You then become convinced of the doctor's explanation when the medication results in lowering your blood glucose level, as predicted by the medical practitioner. But you may not know that you are missing information that provides a more logical explanation.

Under these conditions, I cannot advise you to keep looking on your own for missing information related to your health, even though the more you can understand the medical science behind these lifestyle conditions, the more informed your choices will be. Instead, my suggestion is that the possibility of missing information related to a specific health condition of yours should come from your healthcare provider. In other words, the more questions you ask your provider, the more likely you can fill in the gaps in information you are missing.

In this regard, I believe we need to address the way medical students are taught to speak to and educate not only illiterate patients but also literate ones. For example, doctors are taught the importance of patient autonomy and allow them to make up their minds after explaining the available medical research and guidelines of medical management, mindful of the belief that it is unethical to tell their patients what to do based on their opinion.

This approach assumes that the patient has enough knowledge of the health condition to make up his or her mind. But in my view, while it is important for patients to be involved in their care, medical practitioners should be encouraged not only to share their personal opinions, but also to openly acknowledge when medical science does not have clear answers to the problem at hand.

For example, with high blood sugar and diabetes, doctors should acknowledge that they simply do not yet have proof to explain insulin resistance or why, even with medications that lower blood sugar, patients still incur the serious repercussions of diabetes. Why would there be such inconsistency? In addition, if there are other explanations and treatment possibilities, doctors should have the training to explain these frankly to patients, without having to feel morally responsible for the patient's decision or the fear of being sued for malpractice if something goes wrong. Patients are likely to be happier with their care when providers give honest opinions in a way that is nonjudgmental.

It is also important for doctors to encourage their patients to feel free to ask questions regarding the reliability of any information provided, while acknowledging the fact that medical information and practices based on prevailing concepts are subject to change from time to time. People should be warned periodically to use a critical eye and ear towards health information received, regardless of the source, to find the truth.

One major drawback of this recommendation is the possibility of caregivers becoming inundated with patients bringing loads and loads of questions based on misinformation they receive from the internet and social media.

For the present, even if you have not studied biology since high school, try to learn enough to go ever deeper into the science of the human body so you can assess whether your perceptions and assumptions about diabetes, cancer, and cardiovascular issues may be based on insufficient information. Be open to reading more on those topics of interest to you due to your family history, your age, your history of disease, and your current health status. Challenge your assumptions and be willing to change your views if you find good science that contradicts what you had believed before.

Remember that science changes periodically as researchers gather new data and draw new conclusions to issues they thought they had understood before. This is why we are all missing information if we do not keep reading and learning. Gaining knowledge is a perpetual motion machine; you cannot stop learning. When it comes to lifestyle choices, it is up to you to choose how you want to live. Will your choice be to live as healthfully as possible?

Proposal for Reducing Health Care Costs

Two basic requirements or needs for protecting one's health are accessibility to reliable information and to affordable care. These are both vulnerabilities that could readily be exploited by dreamers, thinkers, and entrepreneurs, based on their level of greed. Although the actions of dreamers, thinkers, and risk takers may advance science and technology, without greed, entrepreneurs are unlikely to risk capital to take chances on production and distribution of new remedies. Since everyone cannot live off the land, there has to be a mechanism to balance the greed of the entrepreneurs with the needs of the common people.

Humans have been designing different systems of governance to balance the interaction between need and greed. Although one can identify faults in every system, democratic capitalism appears to be much more capable, in the long-term, to achieve periodic rebalancing than any other governing system known to humans. So, the question is how we can rebalance the current exorbitant costs of healthcare in the U.S. between greed and need. Although there are many aspects to managing one's health such as nutrition, transportation, etc., in this section I want to concentrate on how we can reduce the costs associated with lifestyle conditions.

Periodic Assessment of Health Care and Costs

By definition, lifestyle-associated health conditions are modifiable through lifestyle changes. This opens up enormous opportunities to exploit vulnerable people with promises of testing, treatments, and prevention. A significant number of people may not have the critical thinking skills needed to evaluate each and every claim, and thus end up choosing a path based on expectations, expediency, or personal beliefs. Popular and political pressure often allow healthcare systems to compensate practitioners of heavily promoted unverified remedies, unnecessarily adding to our healthcare costs. One of the major drawbacks of the current healthcare compensation system, in my opinion, is the lack of a formal periodic assessment of healthcare and associated costs relative to the promised benefits, especially those associated with lifestyle conditions.

To remedy this, I propose the following idea. Every twenty years, there should be a formal review of healthcare procedures and expenditures related to lifestyle conditions. The reason for this is to take into account the potential of new information directly impacting the testing, treatment, and prevention of lifestyle conditions. In this timeframe, there is likely to be new interpretations that expose the need to make changes in the existing methods of identification, treatment, and prevention of one or more lifestyle conditions. There may be better methods available to accomplish the objectives of identifying, treating, and preventing a condition compared to those that are currently being paid for by public and private health insurance programs. This review can be generally classified under three categories: Testing, Treatment, and Prevention.

Testing: We should reevaluate tests that have been previously approved to detect the causes of each of the most common lifestyle conditions: Type 2 diabetes, obesity, cancer, and heart disease. There are two main objectives of such a reevaluation: first, to assess the effectiveness of the available tests to correctly identify the lifestyle condition the test is being conducted for; secondly, to identify critical opportunities that could be helpful in formulating more effective preventive measures.

Treatment: We should assess not only the overall result of treatments that the healthcare system pays for, but also identify any subgroups of people who may benefit from the treatment, even when the results in general are not positive. Assessment of current treatments of lifestyle conditions could also identify those who may experience reduced effectiveness of available treatments due to the presence of interfering agents such as drugs or coexisting conditions or genetic variations.

Prevention: Every twenty years, we should also evaluate any new evidence related to the causative factors of lifestyle conditions so that better preventive measures could be formulated. This could also help identify methods of more effective communication to the most vulnerable populations regarding testing, treatment, and prevention.

Educating the Public

The value of this periodic review is not only to inform legislators, policy makers, and the medical community, but also the lay public. In general, most members of the public have no concept of the true cost of the healthcare they receive. For example, according to National Health Accounts data, U.S. healthcare spending grew 9.7 percent in 2020, reaching $4.1 trillion or $12,530 per person, which, on average, is double as much per person than Switzerland, the country with the second highest per capita health spending. As a share of the nation's Gross Domestic Product, healthcare spending alone accounted for 19.7 percent.

Even those who may be aware of the cost may not know what is responsible for this level of expenditure by the U.S. government. To correct this, what is needed, in my view, is a Senate committee hearing similar to what Sen. George McGovern chaired in 1977 that investigated the increasing incidence of heart attacks experienced by Americans. That hearing resulted in a directive considered to be the precursor of the more detailed "Dietary Guidelines for Americans," the federal review of nutrition and health that is now published every five years.

A similar hearing can be used as a forum to educate the public about the complexities involved in research, development, manufacturing, and marketing of procedures, medications, and gadgets, with testimony from each of the entities contributing to the total expenditures in healthcare.

In such a hearing, researchers and healthcare industry professionals would have to explain how they decide the type of test needed to identify a lifestyle condition; how they conduct research to evaluate the usefulness of the test; and what criteria they use to submit the test for official approval. Researchers would also explain treatments and prevention strategies in a similar fashion. Federal regulators can explain the criteria they use for approval and what mechanisms are used to ensure that the test, treatment, or prevention method meets stated expectations and what safeguards are in place for early detection of potentially harmful side effects that may appear later during the course of the treatment or even afterwards. Manufacturers can explain the cost and effort involved in producing, distributing, and educating not only caregivers but also the public about the benefits of their products and procedures. Medical practitioners can then explain their experience related to compliance by patients regarding adherence to treatment recommendations and behavior modification. Other experts can then shed light on the long-term impact of recommendations related to each of the lifestyle conditions in terms of compliance and results.

For example, if weight reduction programs intended to reduce the incidence of Type 2 diabetes are not successful, experts can inform the committee and the public whether this is due to shortcomings in the programs or to the inability of participants to sustain willpower. Either way, experts can then suggest alternate or modified programs to be tested at different locations to formulate more effective methods to improve the outcomes.

This type of hearing not only allows ordinary people to understand the time, money, and dedication that goes into the production of each test, treatment, and method of prevention for protecting their health, but also what each individual can do to reduce their own healthcare costs and the overall costs paid through their taxes.

Such periodic hearings make it possible to weed out spending taxpayer money on tests, treatments, and prevention programs that do not improve the quality of life, prolong lifespan, or lower the incidence of complications in lifestyle conditions. It also gives an opportunity to warn providers and promoters of services that, if they do not show significant benefits within a specified period of time, they could face a reduction or even termination of remuneration from Medicare, Medicaid, and other government-sponsored health services. Codification of these committee recommendations with instructions for Health and Human Services to create a mechanism for periodic reviews by the legislature along with penalties for repeated non-compliance would, in my opinion, be a better way to rein in rising healthcare costs than piecemeal actions such as forcing companies to reduce the cost of drugs, which, at best, leads only to short-term savings.

Chapter 6 Takeaways

- To protect lives and prevent financial ruin, the U.S. needs a comprehensive and detailed plan to prepare the public and the nation for the next pandemic. The chapter contains 10 strategies to ensure that our health officials are prepared to avoid the spread of disinformation about pandemics. We cannot tolerate any infiltration of disinformation, misinformation, or missing information such as that which has been so prevalent during the Covid-19 pandemic due to the massive volume of anti-science and anti-vaccination messaging that irrationally claims to be protecting personal freedoms.
- Before accepting any information related to the cause or treatment of lifestyle conditions as true, stop and analyze whether the information clearly demonstrates three components: it is logical, has a clearly defined mechanism, and is based on scientific evidence. Every explanation of how a medical illness or condition occurs needs to fulfill these requirements to be acceptable.

- To prevent DMMI from causing you to make bad healthcare decisions, evaluate any messenger who is delivering information to the public. Does the messenger have the capability or training to clearly understand what they are promoting? Does the presenter attempt to discuss a complex topic, yet have no background or education in those areas? Does the presenter exaggerate a claim or fail to clarify exactly what a medication or supplement does? In short, you have to keep in mind that any supposedly reliable source that you have come to accept may not be reliable at all times. They could represent vested interests that are promulgating one or more forms of DMMI.
- Websites and social media can be the source of substantial disinformation and misinformation, promoted by people with vested interests, by criminals and malicious actors, by foreign agents attempting to sow discord in this country, and by adults and kids just playing on people's gullibility. When using the internet and social media, it is important to develop the habit of being constantly on your guard. Use critical thinking: You must ask yourself, does this make logical sense? Does it jive with what you already know about science? Does it reflect a "conspiracy" theory that goes against logic and all evidence? Especially check to see if the information comes from a source that has a vested interest in selling you a product.

EPILOGUE

THE PRIMARY GOAL of healthcare is to help people live longer and better in terms of health and survival. In general, the health status of a patient can be assessed by the individual's symptom burden consisting of the frequency of symptoms a patient may experience as a manifestation of disease or due to their medical treatment and related side-effects; the individual's functional status consisting of physical, emotional, and social function; and the person's health-related quality of life, consisting of the patient's perception of the impact of the disease on health and well-being.

To accomplish the valid societal goal of having quality healthcare that does not sap a nation of its families and workforce population nor its financial resources to pay for healthcare costs, we must work towards having a literate public who can understand the complex issues of good health—such as diet and exercise—but also the nature of lifestyle-generated conditions, and the origins and treatment of illness and disease. We know that prevention is the best approach to control health, especially lifestyle conditions. A large part of prevention is literacy.

We need the literacy of both providers and patients to optimize good health and survival. For this to be successful, providers need to know the exact cause of a lifestyle condition that has been validated through logic, the mechanism by which it affects the body, scientifically confirmed methods of intervention, measurements to assess the value of interventions, and a strategy for modification of each one of these approaches. The public needs to be able to understand the science behind good health, lifestyle conditions, and disease and illness.

There is no doubt that DMMI interferes with literacy. When the public is intentionally fed disinformation or misinformation, or fails to obtain critical missing information, health suffers. Since television, the internet, and social media platforms now function as the public square in which the proliferation of unverified preventive and therapeutic claims is rampant, we must create new systems to give people access to the information they need while alerting them to how DMMI may be leading them to make bad healthcare decisions.

It is estimated that nearly 7 in 10 adults in the United States use Facebook almost daily, with more than a third using it to get their news. This is where many citizens go first to get news about health conditions, express their own views and experiences on remedies tried, and learn about how these impacted others. The challenge is how to accomplish widespread dissemination and access to useful information while not prohibiting free speech that forms the core ideal of a free society and has become a dominant infrastructure of communication. We all may want a platform to express our views and participate without fear of repercussions, but is it in society's interests to allow someone to promote unverified or even harmful content? Is it against freedom to reprimand, temporarily suspend, or banish someone from a media platform if a person persistently promotes false content?

In today's world, it is far too easy for people to claim they are experts on a topic when they actually have no valid credentials or science expertise. For example, it is a common practice during conventions of prestigious medical societies to allow poster or oral presentations by aspiring researchers and to have information on evolving medical technologies and therapeutic modalities presented by various invited participants. Suppose a presenter then uses the act of presenting in this prestigious setting as validation of the effectiveness of the remedy he or she presented? People who learn about the presentation may have no firm knowledge about the claim but can spread it around as being credible because it was delivered at a prestigious conference.

Government and the legal profession might be able to work at creating laws protecting the public from disinformation and misinformation, making it possible to sue people who promote these. But such laws need to be enforceable in the courts. For example, it is currently possible that if one can prove monetary loss, physical injury, damage to property or reputation, or severe emotional stress, the courts could award compensation under some current laws to victims of product failures, accidents, and medical malpractice.

But can we create similar laws to prohibit intentional attempts by an individual or an organization to promote false credentials as a self-proclaimed expert who then touts false health information or unproven remedies? Similarly, what if someone sustains injury after following a remedy suggested by an expert with impressive but fake certificates from a well-known university or someone with impressive credentials from an unaccredited educational institution?

What if the patient suffers damage not because the physician committed malpractice by deviating from practice guidelines but because he or she followed the guidelines that were based on misinterpretation of medical evidence? Who is responsible: the physician for following the guidelines without taking time to clearly understand them, or the medical society that should have changed the guidelines after not obtaining valid scientific evidence to sustain them, even after decades of research, as is the case with insulin resistance-based guidelines to treat Type 2 diabetes?

The fact is, through premium subscriptions, merchandise sales, endorsements, and advertisements, the creators of disinformation make money, regardless of the absence of truth or transparency. They need to be regulated and disincentivized. With the right laws, if a specific harm can be proven in a court of law, victims could get justice.

To start the elimination of disinformation and misinformation, I suggest that the various social media platforms start the process by joining together and appointing a Health Equity Advocacy League

(HEAL) containing academics, researchers, analysts, care providers, and specialists from various local community groups with three specific objectives:

1. To act as expert guardians available to comment when information is presented to promote a product or remedy for a medical condition or when a piece of information related to a specific health condition is spreading rapidly or when readers ask for opinions regarding specific posts.
2. To annotate any comments posted on social media as verified or not, and if verified, to help readers decide how to react.
3. To ensure that health information systems—international, national, and local—have the reach and financial capability to disseminate accurate vital health information, community by community, not only regarding treatments but also methods of prevention.

Practitioners of medical care can then refer patients to HEAL to decide the validity of the information they have regarding their lifestyle condition.

Information—Health—DMMI

While the trajectory of research and innovation in science is often shaped by accidents, foresight, and luck, the practice of medical science is constantly challenged by disinformation, misinformation, and missing information. Your search for information that can help you live a healthy life could expose you to DMMI, both from trusted old sources and new unfamiliar ones.

As I said in the opening of this book, my goal has been to be a patient advocate and shed light on how DMMI can lead millions of people to make poor or wrong choices concerning decisions about simple things such as diet and eating habits, as well as the avoidance of emerging pandemics and the treatment of potentially severe diseases. I hope I have achieved this goal and inspired you to be more mindful of the potential influence of DMMI while making your healthcare decisions so that you can lead a healthy life without Type 2 diabetes, cancer, and heart disease.

My final recommendation is for you to recognize that you are still in charge of your health. Your genetic inheritance, family history, and cultural habits do not create your health destiny. You can build your immune system, overcome illnesses, and avoid lifestyle conditions through your own choices. Don't let DMMI infiltrate your efforts to create your health literacy.

APPENDIX: QUESTIONS TO ASK YOUR DOCTOR

This Appendix provides questions that you can ask your doctor about the lifestyle conditions covered in the chapters of this book. The goal of these questions is not to embarrass your doctor but to help you gain a clearer understanding of the real medical science about your condition and its treatment. However, some of these questions may challenge your doctor to also question whether what he or she believes is accurate. This is potentially an opportunity for your doctor to update his or her knowledge on the topic and even to rethink your treatment plan. Doctors are not right all the time, and sometimes patients must challenge them to go deeper in their understanding of the cause of a lifestyle condition and how best to help you prevent or eliminate it. The questions below are ones whose answers are in this book. If you believe your doctor is not answering the questions well enough, I encourage you to gift them with a copy of this book.

Chapter 1: Pandemics

1. How do masks work? How can I find a mask that works best for me?
2. Can I get an infection by getting vaccinated with the same virus?
3. Why do some people get infection even after getting vaccinated?

4. Do I have to take Covid vaccine every year?
5. Why do children experience less severe Covid symptoms?

Chapter 2: Type 2 Diabetes

1. How do oral medication reduce the glucose in my blood?
2. What is the reason for my body to resist insulin?
3. Is there a test to know the degree of my insulin resistance?
4. My friend needs dialysis in spite of taking insulin. Will I have to do the same?
5. Will my children develop diabetes? Have they discovered a gene for diabetes?

Chapter 3: Body Weight, Diets, and Eating for Nutrition

1. I have normal blood glucose and cholesterol. My brother who is shorter and weighs less than me needs medicines to control blood sugar and cholesterol. Can you explain why?
2. If I already have energy stored as fat, why do I feel hungry?
3. When hungry, I eat almost the same amount of food to feel full. My toddler child eats varying amounts at each meal. Can you explain this?
4. Is it better to eat smaller meals several times per day compared to fasting for longer periods to control my weight?
5. Do you think exercise can prevent obesity and diabetes, even in an older person who has less muscle mass?

Chapter 4: Cancer

1. It is told that gene mutations cause cancer in adults. Is this true for children too?
2. If cancer cells naturally occur in the body all the time, can we cure cancer?

3. I am a cancer survivor. How can I slow the growth of any cancer cells that may still be present in my body?
4. Can I improve my immune system to fight cancer by consuming a wide range of nutritious foods?
5. Will my children inherit cancer genes?

Chapter 5: Cardiovascular Disease

1. Can you explain the role of good (HDL) cholesterol? What does it actually do?
2. What happens to the cholesterol that is removed from my blood when I take a cholesterol lowering medication? Where does it go?
3. Can I consume bran from grain and get the benefits of whole grain?
4. Can't I get the same nutrients as I do in grains from the bran of seeds and nuts?
5. I have high blood pressure, but I still enjoy salty foods. Is it possible to still enjoy foods if I gradually reduce the food salt content slowly?

ENDNOTES

1 https://www.proliteracy.org/Adult-Literacy-Facts

2 https://www.thelancet.com/journals/lancet/article/PIIS0140-6736(20)30183-5/fulltext

3 https://www.washingtonpost.com/opinions/2021/03/04/covid-trump-xi-josh-rogin/

4 https://www.washingtonpost.com/national-security/asian-american-violence/2021/03/19/ea373c52-8839-11eb-bfdf-4d36dab83a6d_story.html

5 https://www.washingtonpost.com/health/2020/12/05/coronavirus-misinformation-facts/

6 https://news.stanford.edu/2020/09/24/covid-19-spread-american-prisons/

7 https://www.nationalgeographic.com/history/article/how-cities-flattened-curve-1918-spanish-flu-pandemic-coronavirus

8 https://www.sciencedaily.com/releases/2020/08/200821155737.htm

9 https://abcnews.go.com/Politics/study-finds-earlier-coronavirus-restrictions-us-saved-36k/story?id=70808611

10 Arteriosclerosis and Diabetes. Elliot P. Joslin, Annals of Clinical Medicine, vol V 1927

11 https://clinical.diabetesjournals.org/content/20/1/45.short#:~:text=Self%2Dmonitoring%20of%20blood%20glucose%20(SMBG)%20is%20an%20important,control%20and%20to%20prevent%20hypoglycemia.

12 https://allulose.org/author/ssamples/page/8/

13 *Prevalence of Chronic Complications, Their Risk Factors, and the Cardiovascular Risk Factors among Patients with Type 2 Diabetes Attending the Diabetic Clinic at a Tertiary Care Hospital in Sri Lanka.* Journal of Diabetes Research, May 2018: M.H. Arambevela et al.

14 Davis, CM. 1928, Self-selection of diet by newly weaned infants. An experimental study. The American Journal of Diseases of Children. 36:651-679.

15 *Marked improvement in carbohydrate and lipid metabolism in diabetic Australian aborigines after temporary reversion to traditional lifestyle*, Kerin O'Dea. Diabetes. 1984 Jun;33(6):596-603. doi: 10.2337/diab.33.6.596.

16 *It is time to bust the myth of physical inactivity and obesity: you cannot outrun a bad diet.* A Malhotra, T. Noakes, S. Phinney. British Journal of Sports Medicine 2015: Vol 49, Issue 5.

17 Theobald, D. L. (May 2010). "A formal test of the theory of universal common ancestry". Nature. 465(7295): 219–222.

18 European Society of Cardiology, August 25, 2018: *Too much of a good thing? Very high levels of 'good' cholesterol may be harmful.*

19 https://efsa.onlinelibrary.wiley.com/doi/pdf/10.2903/j.efsa.2010.1766

20 *A COVID vaccine grown in plants measures up*, NPR broadcast, December 7, 2021

21 Reduced Risk of Reinfection with SARS-CoV-2 After COVID-19 Vaccination — Kentucky, May–June 2021, *Weekly*, August 13, 2021 / 70(32); 1081-1083. On August 6, 2021, this report was posted online as an MMWR Early Release.

ABOUT THE AUTHOR

Dr. John Poothullil, MD, FCRP

Dr. Poothullil practiced medicine as a pediatrician and allergist for more than 30 years, with 27 of those years in the state of Texas. He received his medical degree from the University of Kerala, India in 1968, after which he completed two years of medical residency in Washington, D.C., and Phoenix, Arizona and two years of fellowship, one in Milwaukee, Wisconsin and the other in Ontario, Canada. He began his practice in 1974 and retired in 2008. He holds certifications from the American Board of Pediatrics, The American Board of Allergy & Immunology, and the Canadian Board of Pediatrics.

During his medical practice, John became interested in understanding the causes of and interconnections between hunger, satiation, and weight gain. His interest turned into a passion and a multi-decade personal study and research project that led him to read many medical journal articles, medical textbooks, and other scholarly works in biology, biochemistry, physiology, endocrinology, and cellular metabolic functions. This eventually guided Dr. Poothullil to investigate the theory of insulin resistance as it relates to diabetes. Recognizing that this theory was illogical, he spent several years rethinking the biology behind high blood sugar and developed the fatty acid burn theory as the real cause of diabetes.

He then continued researching the linkage between diabetes and cancer and developed additional insights into the causes of childhood and adult cancer and possible treatments involving low-carbohydrate diets to initiate starving of cancer cells by removing their main source of energy — glucose from grains.

Dr. Poothullil has written articles on hunger and satiation, weight loss, diabetes, and the senses of taste and smell. His articles have been published in medical journals such as *Physiology and Behavior, Neuroscience and Biobehavioral Reviews, Journal of Women's Health, Journal of Applied Research, Nutrition,* and *Nutritional Neuroscience.* His work has also been quoted in *Woman's Day, Fitness, Red Book* and *Woman's World.* His articles on diabetes have been published in *Alternative Medicine, Whole Person, India Abroad,* and several other magazines.

Dr. Poothullil has published four books, two of which have won publishing awards in national book competitions.

- *Eat Chew Live: 4 Revolutionary Ideas to Prevent Diabetes, Lose Weight & Enjoy Food* (Over & Above Creative, 2015) — Winner, Beverly Hills Book Awards, Nutrition Category 2016
- *Diabetes: The Real Cause and the Right Cure: 8 Steps to Reverse Type 2 Diabetes in 8 Weeks* (New Insights Press, 2017) — Finalist, Beverly Hills Books Awards, Diet & Nutrition Category 2017
- *Surviving Cancer: A New Perspective on Why Cancer Happens & Your Key Strategies for a Healthy Life* (New Insights Press, 2017)
- *When Your Child Has Cancer: Insights and Information to Empower Parents* (New Insights Press, 2020)

Dr. Poothullil is an active speaker on diabetes and cancer. He has appeared on four television shows, interviewed on over 60 national and local radio programs, and given more than 40 talks to groups in bookstores and private groups and associations. An interview with him appeared in the Washington Post. He has published nearly 130 blogs on his website *www.DrJohnOnHealth.com.*

Dr. Poothullil is the health consultant for the nationally syndicated AM radio talk show, *America's First News*, hosted by Matt Ray. He speaks every Tuesday morning on the show, which is broadcast in over 100 stations across the US.

Other Books by John Poothullil, MD, FRCP

For people who are interested in preventing Type 2 Diabetes

Eat Chew Live: 4 Revolutionary Ideas to Prevent Diabetes, Lose Weight and Enjoy Food by Dr. Poothullil is a comprehensive guide in preventing diabetes. It goes into extensive detail about the lack of logic with the insulin resistance theory, why the fatty acid burn theory makes more sense to understand the cause of high blood sugar and Type 2 diabetes, and what everyone can do to change their thinking and eating habits to ensure they do not develop high blood sugar and diabetes.

WINNER, 2016 BEVERLY HILLS BOOKS AWARDS

OVER AND ABOVE PRESS

Available in print and ebook format on Amazon and in Bookstores

Information about Reversing Type 2 Diabetes

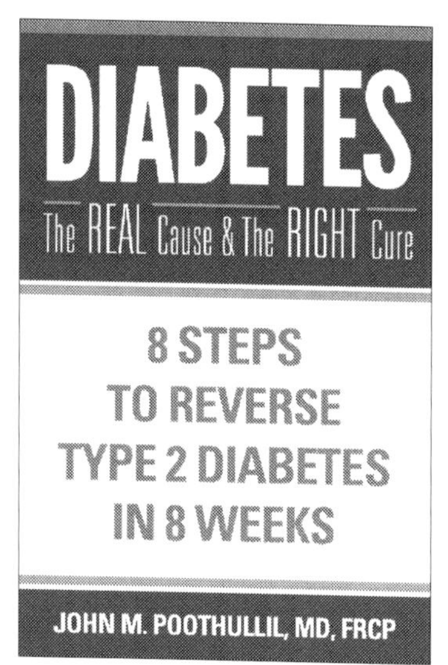

Unless YOU do something about it, your diabetes will be a progressive disease because medication and insulin injections do not reverse it. This book provides NEW INSIGHT that will lower blood sugar and halt your diabetes. Based on twenty years studying the scientific research ondiabetes, Dr. Poothullil shows that the theory of insulin resistance cannot be valid. The REAL cause of diabetes is the consumption of grains and grain products. The RIGHT cure for diabetes is not medication or insulin injections, but altering your diet.

Warning: Insulin injections and insulin-releasing medications make no sense if you are supposedly insulin resistant. In fact, these are endangering you:

- Insulin makes you hungry so you eat more and gain weight, making your diabetes worse
- Insulin injections lower blood sugar, but they do not prevent diabetic complications— damage to nerve cells, blindness, kidney failure, and atherosclerosis—and could cause abnormally low blood sugar which could be life-threatening
- Insulin promotes cancer cell growth, which is why there is a higher incidence of cancer among people with diabetes than those without Don't risk having Type 2 diabetes for the rest of your life, regardless of your age or how long you have had it. Learn how to reverse diabetes using 8 simple steps in 8 weeks so you can restore your health.

Don't risk having Type 2 diabetes for the rest of your life, regardless of your age or how long youhave had it. Learn how to reverse diabetes using 8 simple steps in 8 weeks so you can restore your health.

New Insights Press

Available in print and ebook format on Amazon and in Bookstores

Information about Cancer in Children

If you are the parent of a child with cancer, the overwhelming multitude of questions, feelings, and associated anxieties are hard to contain. What caused the cancer? What can you as a parent do to help your child live through it? What is the future for your child?

In this insightful and thoughtful book, you will find information, hope, advice, and solace. Dr. John Poothullil expertly guides you to understand childhood cancer. He starts with his two new scientific theories to explain how the leading types of childhood cancers might occur, given that children have not lived long enough to develop the number of gene mutations that usually cause adult cancers.

You will learn how you as parents can care for your child with cancer with understanding and sensitivity, creating a loving home environment full of communal activities to reduce everyone's stress and worry.

Most importantly, Dr. Poothullil explains why your child's diet can be a key corollary element in controlling cancer along with the medical treatments. You will learn how a diet low in grains and grain-flour products slows cancer cell growth, giving your child's immune system a better chance to contain it.

Valuable extra material in the book includes simple instructions to do gardening and cooking as calming activities to enjoy life for children with cancer. Three superbly illustrated short stories that parents can share with their child are also included.

"Well-written and well-explained... Dr. Poothullil's reasons for addressing dietary issues are clear and compelling.... Well worth a careful reading."

—PETER C. PHILLIPS, MD, Pediatric Oncologist

New Insights Press

Available in print and ebook format on Amazon and in Bookstores

Made in the USA
Middletown, DE
08 May 2022

65194482R00135